# Leading and Managing Strategic Suppliers

# Leading and Managing Strategic Suppliers

Richard Moxham

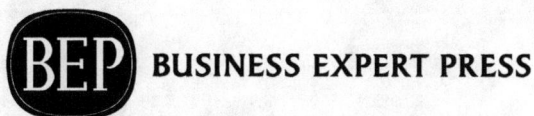

BEP BUSINESS EXPERT PRESS

*Leading and Managing Strategic Suppliers*
Copyright © Business Expert Press, LLC, 2019.

First published in 2019 by
Business Expert Press, LLC
222 East 46th Street, New York, NY 10017
www.businessexpertpress.com

ISBN-13: 978-1-94819-866-0 (paperback)
ISBN-13: 978-1-94819-867-7 (e-book)

Business Expert Press Supply and Operations Management Collection

Collection ISSN: 2156-8189 (print)
Collection ISSN: 2156-8200 (electronic)

Cover and interior design by S4Carlisle Publishing Services Private Ltd., Chennai, India

First edition: 2019

10 9 8 7 6 5 4 3 2 1

Printed in the United States of America.

# Abstract

Strategic suppliers provide critical products and services to their clients. If the supply chain for key components breaks down and the components do not arrive on the contracted just-in-time (JIT) date, then the whole production line may stop. If an IT supplier fails to deliver key system development projects on time, the implications for the effectiveness of core business processes can be catastrophic. With the growth of outsourcing, where whole business functions are delegated to a supplier, the dependency on them is further increased. When the outsource is to a supplier in a different geography, remote from the client, the additional complexities and challenges of outsourcing—for example, remote communications, different cultures—must be managed. An organization's ability to manage its strategic supplier base effectively is central to its performance, competitiveness, and future success.

This book provides practical guidance on the knowledge and skills required for managers whose role involves the management of the relationship with and the performance of strategically important suppliers. While the focus is on the management of suppliers during the live relationship after procurement, the approach is holistic as the entire supplier management process is discussed in detail using a Supplier Lifecycle model. The model describes five clear stages—identify the business requirement for the services to be provided, research the supply market, carry out procurement and supplier selection, integrate and transition to the new supplier and services to the organization, manage the delivery of the products and services for the contracted period, including the supplier responses to changing customer needs.

# Key words

strategic suppliers; outsourcing; offshoring; supplier management; supplier relationship management; service delivery management; supplier lifecycle; supplier performance management; managing cross-cultural supplier relationships

# Contents

# Acknowledgments

The contents of this book are based on the knowledge and experience I have built up in my business career, and latterly, in the last 15 years, facilitating supplier manager workshops for many clients, involving, over the period, hundreds of participants. While my role in those workshops was to facilitate learning, the interactive nature of the events, and the discussions with participants, all of whom were involved in managing suppliers, meant that the learning was not just one way—I learned a lot from the people I met. So, my acknowledgment and thanks to those people, far too many to mention by name, who are unknowing contributors to this book.

More specifically, my thanks to Martin Webb of Value Dynamics, who I worked with closely on a major public sector engagement some time ago. We exchanged knowledge and experience, and Martin has kindly given me permission to include some of his thinking in the content. Also, my thanks to Loes Hasain-Cornelissen of Geert Hofstede BV for her support and guidance in refining and finalizing the content of the chapter on cross-cultural working. In addition, I would like to express my gratitude to the people and organizations that contributed to the content by granting permission to reference their published works.

Finally, I would like to acknowledge the support of my wife, Susan, and Sarah, my daughter. Sarah kept me focused by relentlessly reminding me of the deadlines I had set myself and was, at times, in danger of missing. Susan became the quality control manager, frequently critiquing my terminology and grammar and demonstrating the highest level of proofreading skills.

# CHAPTER 1

# Introduction

## Supplier Management: Some Simple Truths

There is an old saying that not all customers are equal; by the same token, not all suppliers are equal. Therefore, supplier management is not one thing, as there will be different approaches and processes driven by how the customer categorizes specific suppliers, ranging from very transactional to long-term partnerships. The management of strategic suppliers is of key importance, and these suppliers form the focus of this book. Put simply, strategic suppliers are important because what they provide is essential to the successful operation of the business. The consequences of nondelivery or poor service delivery are serious, and typically, but not always, customers spend a lot of money with such suppliers

## The Growth of Outsourcing

While not all strategic suppliers provide outsource services, generally suppliers of outsource services tend to fall into the strategic category. Hence, outsourcing, and the management of such relationships, figures highly in this book. Over the last 30 years or so there has been a massive growth in the outsourcing of mission critical services by corporates, educational establishments, utilities, and the total spectrum of public sector organizations. The term *mission critical services* is a broad-based one as it can cover information technology (IT), facilities management, customer services, and business process outsourcing (BPO) involving functions such as back office/administrative, human resources (HR), and logistics. At the same time, we have seen the continued rise of globalization, so given this phenomenon, offshoring has become a major part of their outsourcing strategy for many organizations. The estimated value of the global outsourcing market for 2017—$88.9 billion—is a good indicator of the size of the market (source: Statistica.com).

Given the time that outsourcing has existed, and the scale of the market, it would be reasonable to assume that, as a business sector, it has reached maturity. If you search "why does outsourcing fail" it takes Google 5 seconds to come back with 1,098,000 results. A meaningless figure? However, it does suggest that outsourcing does not work for all customers. As a key stated driver for outsourcing is to engage with experts in their sector, allowing the client (outsourcer) to focus on their core business, the delivery of excellent service levels should be a given, should it not? This is not to decry outsourcing and the value it can bring to organizations. I make the point for one key reason: Managing strategic, often outsourcing, relationships is a complex task. It requires sound planning, robust processes, and excellent interpersonal skills. Possibly, the reasons for dissatisfaction can be a result of the way strategic supplier and outsourcing decisions are made and how those relationships are subsequently managed, rather than the idea of outsourcing itself. There is clear evidence that if the processes of supplier selection are sound, and if the skills and experience exist to effectively manage supplier performance and relationship, then those suppliers can become effective partners to the business by providing cost-effective solutions, process improvements, and end user satisfaction.

## Setting the Context for Strategic Supplier Management

First, it is important to establish the focus and objectives of this book.

The *primary* focus is on the postprocurement phase of the overall supplier engagement. The *main* objective is to provide practical guidance and learning for those people in an organization whose job includes responsibility for the management of the performance of and the relationship with suppliers. I will come back to the use of the words *primary* and *main* later in this chapter.

Having established the focus, we now provide the context. The management of the performance of and relationship with the engaged supplier is only part of a bigger process that includes, for example, defining the business requirements the supplier must address, researching the supplier marketplace, completing the procurement process, and drawing up contracts. This overall process is defined in the supplier lifecycle model, which is covered in detail in Chapter 2. The stages in the lifecycle helped determine the structure and sequence of the chapters in this book.

In studying the stages in the lifecycle, it will become clear that a number of functions and job roles will be involved in different stages of the journey. For example, business analysts will have a role in requirements definition; the purchasing team in the tendering process; the legal team in drawing up the contract, assessing risk, and ensuring due diligence; HR where staff are being transferred to the supplier organization—and I have not yet mentioned the people responsible for managing the supplier once engaged.

Having a clearly defined lifecycle as a map and guide is vital. There is, however, potentially a problem. That is, the stages in the lifecycle are often treated like silos, with the relevant function involved in their part of the process in isolation. This can mean that the subject matter experts (SMEs) do not have enough involvement in procurement, so decisions become very purchasing interest centric; this can mean that users (end customers) are not consulted sufficiently at the requirements definition stage so that the practical considerations and challenges are lost; this can mean that the people who ultimately will have to manage the live relationship are not sufficiently involved or briefed on the contract or the transitioning stages through to deliver, and business as usual (BAU).

I have stated "the people responsible for the performance of and relationship with the engaged supplier" a couple of times already in this introduction. Let me introduce a further complication—in all my years with many organizations, running seminars and workshops on supplier management, I have never seen or heard of a one-size-fits-all generic supplier manager job role. This is because there is not one but several different roles in the live delivery phase. Typical job titles include supplier relationship manager, supplier delivery manager, contracts manager, supplier liaison manager, to name but a few, often with the prefixes of strategic, business, operational to increase the overall number of permutations.

So, I have established that supplier management is part of an overall supplier lifecycle, many different functions are potentially involved at different stages, and even at the postprocurement engaged supplier phase there is more than one role involved.

The key questions, therefore: Who will benefit from reading this book? What job roles is it targeted at?

## Who Will Gain Value from Reading This Book?

Let me return to my use of the words *primary* and *main*.

The *primary* focus is on the postprocurement phase of the overall supplier engagement. The lifecycle, however, covers the end to end supplier journey from requirements definition to eventual exit. For a supplier relationship manager involved in the ongoing relationship, understanding how requirements were defined and by whom, what procurement steps were involved, and what the overall process of supplier selection was and against what criteria the selection was made will help them become more effective in their role. Also, some relationship managers may have a role in procurement anyway, so this stage of the lifecycle could be a primary focus for them. All other steps could fall into secondary focus, or contextual interest. A business analyst will have a far greater in-depth understanding of requirements definition than the coverage in this book—the other chapters are likely to be useful for their overall understanding of supplier management at a contextual level.

The *main* objective is to provide practical guidance and learning for those people in an organization whose job includes responsibility for the management of the performance of and relationship with suppliers. The secondary objective is to provide an understanding of the overall supplier engagement process to anyone whose job involves some supplier management responsibilities at any stage of the lifecycle.

To summarize, I am confident that anyone whose role has some involvement in supplier engagement and management will benefit from the ideas, processes, and skills discussed in the following chapters.

## A Guide to Using This Book

The chapters of this book follow a logical sequence, as described in the supplier lifecycle. There are 17 chapters, including this introductory piece.

For the main target group of this book—those involved in managing the performance of and relationship with a supplier once engaged and the relationship is live—Chapters 1 through 5 cover the front-end stages of the lifecycle, starting with requirements definition through to sourcing. Chapters 6 through 16 cover the lifecycle stages postsourcing/procurement—the management of the performance of and relationship with the supplier. These are the chapters that have the most direct relevance for people involved in managing those live relationships. Chapters 1 through 5 serve as a useful context as they provide insights into the supplier selection process.

The following table provides a brief description of the content of each chapter:

1. Introduction: Setting the context for strategic supplier management, how to get most value from the book.
2. Definitions, lifecycle, and key themes: This is essential reading as the chapter provides the overall road map and describes the key messages and concepts that are developed in subsequent chapters.
3. Defining requirements: At an overview level, this chapter describes the necessary process to ensure that the business requirements are clearly defined for input into the subsequent tender documents—*suggest this is read for context and background understanding.*
4. Research: This provides a comprehensive guide for carrying out supplier market research proactively prior to any formal supplier dialogue—*suggest this is read for context and background understanding.*
5. Sourcing overview: An explanation of the sourcing process is provided at a broad overview level, and it describes in generic terms the steps involved in a typical procurement and supplier selection process—*suggest this is read for context and background understanding.*
6. Contract knowledge and supplier background: An explanation of the essential information required to enable effective supplier performance management; *this and all subsequent chapters are essential reading for anyone involved in managing the live relationship.*
7. Managing internal stakeholders: While the focus is on supplier management, management of internal stakeholders who have an interest in the supplier engagement is equally important.

8. Establishing the working code: This defines how to work with a supplier to develop a positive working relationship on the basis of a number of mutual expectations regarding behavior; in a sense, an *emotional contract*.

9. Cross-cultural working: Offshoring adds in the complexity of remote working and different cultural norms, and thus requires a specifically adapted working code (there is a link to Chapter 8).

10. Supplier communication and influencing: This gives an introduction to a behavioral model based on some of the principles of situational leadership, and specifically how to achieve the balance of directing and engaging with suppliers.

11. Performance review and development: This chapter provides a number of practical tips and checklists , along with the skills required for making reviews positive and engaging, and balancing reviewing past performance with developing the future relationship.

12. Operational negotiation: Not to be confused with contract negotiation, this covers the practicalities of reaching agreements daily or weekly at the operational level on a range of subjects and issues.

13. Managing changing requirements: The one thing for certain is that the requirements, as initially defined, will change. This chapter provides a series of practical checklists, with the supplier manager often behaving as the conduit between the supplier and end customer.

14. Handling conflicts and disputes: While not inevitable, conflicts and disagreements at some point during the period of the contract are likely. This chapter covers the behaviors that are most effective in resolving such situations.

15. Keeping the supplier engaged: This answers a key question—how to ensure that the supplier's commitment and energy at the start of the contract are maintained throughout the period of the contract.

16. Managing the exit: This chapter defines a process for managing the exit and mitigating the additional risks to service delivery during this period.

17. Summary, key messages, summary of reading list, and other resources: This chapter serves as a summary reminder of all the key points covered in the preceding chapters and provides information on additional learning resources.

For those people outside of the key target reader group, you can select the most relevant chapters considering the specific scope and supplier management responsibilities of your job role.

## Style and Structure

The objective is to provide a guide for best practices for managing strategic suppliers. You are busy people, so you may not have time to read heavy text. Written from this perspective, this book has the following features:

- Each chapter starts with a very brief summary of what will be covered.
- Text is supported by practical checklists.
- Toward the end of each chapter there are *thought provoker questions*—useful for those readers whose job role includes managing suppliers. Hopefully, your reflections on the questions will give you some ideas and pointers for developing or changing the current way of working. It may even lead you to stop doing certain things.
- Each chapter concludes with the *key takeaways question*—leading you to think about the things you can consider and/or implement in your organization or for your personal development.

# CHAPTER 2

# Definitions, Lifecycle, and Key Themes

*In this chapter: definition of strategic supplier management, key themes and values that underpin the effective management of strategic suppliers, introduction to and explanation of the IRSID supplier lifecycle model*

## Definition of Strategic Supplier Management

As a starting point, let me give you a definition of strategic supplier management:

> An all-encompassing strategy and plan to create most *value* from the supplier relationship by managing and developing their *performance* using a balanced combination of managing to a clearly defined *contract* while developing positive working *relationships*

If you google *definition of strategic supplier management*, you get 202,000,000 results in 60 seconds, so I am not claiming that mine is the only definition. It is, of course, an incredibly broad definition. In subsequent chapters the detail will be developed and discussed, with specific reference to the four points italicized in the definition—*value, performance, contract, relationship.*

The definition also provides the basis for establishing some key themes that run throughout the stages of the supplier engagement.

## Key Themes

- **Striking a balance between contract and relationship is key to success:** Having a robust contract with clearly defined deliverables is a prerequisite for effective supplier management. This does not mean using the contract as a weapon against the supplier—it should be seen as a protection for both parties. Establishing a strong, positive working relationship is as important as drawing up a robust contract. A balanced combination of the two will result in optimum value.

- **There is a clear link between a positive relationship and good performance:** It is simple, really—if people like you, they are prepared to do more for you. It works in one-to-one relationships; it works with strategic suppliers, because ultimately it is about people and how they get along. It is a commonly held view that the customers with the biggest spend get the most from a supplier. Of course, business reality is that money is important but there are many cases where customers with relatively little spending power get a lot of value because they are easy to work with.

- **Maximizing value from the relationship for both parties is the ultimate goal:** The contract defines what needs to be delivered by the supplier, so in a sense simply by delivering the product or the service, value is being delivered. Maximizing value means something additional, over and above the contractual commitments whereby the customer receives products/services (value) and the supplier receives payment (value). The additional value will only be achieved if both parties see a benefit in investing in the relationship. An example of additional value is where a supplier, outside of the scope of the service they are contracted to deliver, proposes streamlined processes that result in increased efficiencies for the customer.

- **The supplier manager has a representational role:** The purpose of this book is to provide guidance for managing suppliers most effectively. I have lost count of the number of times individuals in supplier manager roles have said to me, "In fact, managing the supplier is often a lot simpler than managing the internal customers and other stakeholders"—an important and very relevant point. The reality is that the supplier manager is the conduit between the supplier and the business, often representing the customer to the supplier and the supplier to the customer. The customer typically sees the supplier manager as the supplier. Many of the tips and ideas we cover in subsequent chapters for managing supplier relationships can be equally applied to managing internal stakeholder relationships.

- **The customer should be an intelligent customer:** The customer has a responsibility to enable the supplier to deliver—as a minimum—to the standards defined in the contract. This is a key concept in underpinning the notion that strategic relationships are genuinely about shared responsibilities. How often have you heard of situations where the supplier is being criticized for not delivering the service they are responsible for, when on investigation, the customer's processes, the lack of clearly defined requirements ,poor decision making (or lack of decisions), continuous change of priorities, or old-fashioned politics prevent the supplier from doing their job? Outsourcing does not include outsourcing of all responsibility.

- **There is often a recognition of mutual dependency:** There is an adage that the pressure to sell is always greater than the pressure to buy. There is a second adage that customer is king, and therefore, holds all the cards. These may have been true in less complex business environments and might still be true where there is a very transactional relationship. When a decision has, however, been made to engage a strategic supplier, possibly on an outsource contract basis, then realistically there emerges a mutual dependency. The level of dependency will depend on a number of factors. At some points in the relationship, and depending on the service being provided, it is possible that the customer will have a greater dependency than the supplier. This is a reality. This does not mean that you hand control to the supplier. It does mean that how the relationship is managed is key.

## The Lifecycle: IRSID

The lifecycle describes the end-to-end supplier management process—starting with defining requirements through to eventually exiting the contract and the supplier. In effect, the lifecycle describes a journey and provides a roadmap for that journey. In addition, it helps those in an operational supplier management role to understand what parts of the supplier journey they are involved in, what other stakeholders are involved, and what is the importance of bridges and links between the phases of the lifecycle.

This five-step process highlights a crucial fact: Supplier management is more than managing a supplier once they have been appointed; supplier management starts when the decision has been made to identify and hire a supplier to provide a product/service or to manage and deliver a project on behalf of the business. As will become clear, the effectiveness of each step in the supplier management journey will be very dependent on the effective completion of the preceding steps.

There are five steps in the lifecycle:

I—**Identify** the requirements, the key feed to the lifecycle.

R—**Research** the supply market, potential suppliers, sourcing strategy.

S—**Source** involves procurement, going to the market, selecting a supplier.

I—**Integrate** involves engaging and transitioning.

D—**Deliver** entails managing the supplier performance and relationship.

What follows is a breakdown and detailing of points for each phase.

## Identify

*Identification of requirements*: If a decision is made to meet those requirements via an external organization, this becomes a feed into the lifecycle.

- Summary of requirements and required outcomes/deliverables
- Business drivers, linking the requirement to strategy
- Detailed specification of requirements at the business, functional, and technical levels
- Clear definition of assumptions, dependencies, and constraints
- Application of business case tests
- Internal/external delivery decision; if external, then a direct feed into the lifecycle

## Research

*Investigation and planning*: These are done before moving to sourcing—to ensure that the strategy is focused on the most effective engagement models with the right *screened in* potential suppliers.

- Technology/solution options
- Regulatory considerations
- Risk analysis—internal and external factors
- Supply market positioning and analysis
- Identification of potential suppliers
- Dialogue with potential suppliers
- Sourcing strategy

## Source

*The formal procurement phase*: This involves going to the market with defined requirements, receiving proposals, and making selection decisions against predefined criteria.

- Issue RFI (request for information)
- RFI response analysis, screen in/out
- Issue RFP (request for proposal) to shortlisted suppliers
- Receipt and analysis of proposals
- Raise queries as necessary
- Potential supplier meetings/presentations
- Initial analysis of suppliers against selection criteria
- Validate supplier claims with references
- Supplier selection—provisional depending on outcomes of contract discussions
- Contract negotiation
- Final decision; communicate decision internally and to other bidders

## Integrate

*Engaging and transitioning*: This is the iterative stage between the sourcing decision and the delivery. It is designed to ensure that people and processes are aligned in moving from the current state to the new business as usual (BAU).

- Clarify/define the teams (client and supplier) that will be involved in the delivery phase.
- Detail the transition plan, and ensure the onboarding (new supplier) and exit (existing supplier) plans are aligned.
- Clarify/establish the stakeholders during the delivery phase and the stakeholder communication plan.
- Clarify with the respective delivery teams the agreed delivery scope and performance measures—SLA (service level agreement), KPIs (key performance indicators), project deliverables.
- Establish the process and timetable for performance review forums.
- Agree on how you are going to work together—establish the working code.

## Deliver

*Implementing and developing*: This step is aimed at ensuring the supplier delivers, as a minimum, what they are contracted to deliver, to quality, time, and price. Developing is about investing in the relationship, to enhance performance, and maximizing value.

- Manage the operational performance.
- Conduct periodic reviews as defined in the governance structure.
- Decisively handle supplier underperformance.
- Manage change, which can be driven by customers and/or suppliers, to ensure that business needs continue to be met.
- Regularly review performance measures, ensuring that the right things are being measured to the right level, and facilitate change as necessary.
- Represent the customer to the supplier and the supplier to the customer.
- Drive the concept of continuous improvement to ensure optimum performance.

- A very specific point—in an exit situation (either contract and/ or supplier is being terminated), it is a key responsibility for the supplier manager and the supplier to ensure that service delivery continues at the agreed contract performance levels.

## Guidelines and Tips for Working with the Model

1. While IRSID is represented as a straightforward, linear, sequential process, in reality it is often more complex and iterative. For example, the view of requirements (I) could be influenced and revised following research into the marketplace and meetings with potential suppliers (R). An initial view on the key performance measures (SLA, KPIs) would be drafted at the requirements stage (I), but could be reviewed after presentation of proposals by suppliers in the sourcing phase (S). The interaction between the transitioning (I) and the delivery (D) phases is likely to be quite high.

2. Related to point (1), it is possible that activities are taking place in different stages of the lifecycle at any given time. For example, a contract may be coming to an end and performance must be maintained during the exit phase (part of D), at the same time as work is being carried out to renew the contract, with refined requirements, with the same or a different supplier (stages I, D, eventually moving into S).

3. Like any such model, the supplier lifecycle should be viewed and used as a guide rather than seen as a straitjacket and a rigid process.

4. In the introductory chapter, I highlighted the risk of the steps in supplier engagement being viewed and actioned with a silo mentality. The lifecycle model can be helpful in mapping who should be involved at each stage, so the necessary bridges and links across the interested functions can be established.

5. The model, and the explanation of the steps in each stage, can be used as a practical checklist to verify if all points have been covered before moving on to the next stage in the process.

### *Thought Provokers*

1. Given your current job role, where are you involved in the supplier lifecycle?

2. Linked to question (1), where do you think it would be beneficial for you to be involved, over and above the answer in (1)?

3. What ideas and suggestions could you provide to colleagues to help the team manage your strategic suppliers more effectively?

## Takeaways

From a personal learning perspective, what are your three key takeaways from this chapter?

| | |
|---|---|
| 1 | |
| 2 | |
| 3 | |

# CHAPTER 3

# Defining Requirements

*In this chapter: the importance of clearly defined requirements, the inclusion of performance levels in requirements, a seven-point template for producing a requirements document*

## The Importance of Clearly Defined Requirements

As a starting point for exploring the importance of clearly defined requirements, I would like to fast-forward to the delivery stage of the lifecycle—the supplier now is hired, is providing the service, and sending monthly invoices. Here are two questions to consider.

First, why is it quite common that the users of the service feel that their needs are not being met? Why do they feel dissatisfied with the service? There are two possible reasons: The first is that the requirements, as stated in the contract, are correct, but the supplier is failing to deliver to the agreed performance standards. The second reason is that the delivery specification, as defined in the contract, is incorrect, which implies that the requirements definition was incorrect or imprecise at the outset. The reality is that customer dissatisfaction can be caused by either reason one or reason two or a combination. Let's hold on to reason two for the moment, and look at the second question.

Why is it, and I am thinking specifically here of IT contracts, that the number and pace of level of change notices is typically high, not just when the contract has been running for a period, but often at the outset of the engagement? Again, there are potentially two reasons: One reason is that the customer requirements are legitimately changing rapidly on an ongoing basis. The other reason is that the change requests are being instigated because the original requirements were incorrect or incomplete. It is likely that change requests are a result of a combination of both reasons.

The logical conclusion is that poorly defined, incomplete, imprecise requirements can lead to customer dissatisfaction and high rates of change requests. Both are clearly negative outcomes, and an overload of change requests is both disruptive and costly. If any proof is needed of the costs involved, it has not been unknown for a savvy supplier to agree to a contract at a less than ideal margin for them, because they know that they will gain in the mid and long term from the additional revenues generated by change requests. Maybe a cynical view, but very true.

The aforementioned points clearly identify the consequences of poorly defined requirements. Having established the case for clearly defined requirements, let us look at the underlying reasons why there is a failure in definition. If the requirements are not correct or complete, then the expected outcomes from the subsequent stages of the lifecycle are doomed to fail—simple and straightforward—for the following reasons:

- The RFP (request for proposal—sometimes called the ITT, invitation to tender) will ask selected potential suppliers to produce proposals for addressing the requirements as stated in the RFP, which would have used the requirements definition document as input.
- There are two possible outcomes from the previous point: Some suppliers may raise questions about the requirements that could uncover deficiencies in the requirements definition; of course, this could be a positive outcome, but it would require a restart of the RFP process—time consuming and costly. The other outcome is that the suppliers provide proposals to address the needs as stated, and one of those proposals is accepted.
- So, we come full circle—contracts are signed, the live engagement starts, customer needs are not met, resulting in customer dissatisfaction and high levels of service change required.

## Seven-Point Template for Requirements Definition Document

1. Executive summary
2. Background and context
3. Business requirements and drivers
4. Scope definition—to include out-of-scope work

5. Minimum performance standards for key areas
6. Dependencies and assumptions
7. Constraints

Think of this template as a *guide* and as a *thought process*.

It is designed to provide an overall context and background, as well as to define in detail what the requirements are.

The documentation you use and its format will depend on which part of the business you are from and whether you are working with service delivery or project-based suppliers—but, in broad terms, the needs definition is a similar process.

Each of the seven points involves a number of subpoints, and these are summarized in the following explanations.

The completed document provides the key feed into the sourcing process and is an integral part of the RFP, which is covered in detail in Chapter 5.

1. Executive summary
   • A high-level description of the requirements
   • The deliverables expected of the supplier
2. Background and context
   • How business requirements have evolved to the present day
   • Current solution—system, process, and so on
   • The degree to which current requirements are being met
   • Any relevant recent history
3. Business requirements and drivers
   • Description of the business requirements proposals must address, including current and those envisaged for the future
   • Description of what needs to be delivered by the supplier
   • Define the factors that are driving the requirement and why they are important.
   • Implications of nondelivery
4. Scope definition
   • Description of the service or project that the supplier must deliver
   • Description should be broken down into key areas, with a detailed description for each of them and a clear statement of the required deliverables.

- Scope must include timelines for completion, and for each stage in the delivery or project plan.
- Out-of-scope work should be clearly defined. This is particularly important as it helps to clarify exactly what is in scope and saves unnecessary work and clarification later.

5. Minimum performance standards for key areas
   - Define minimum performance standards required for key deliverables.
   - The fact that they are minimum requirements should be stressed during the RFP.
   - These can be refined during the engaging process with the selected supplier.

   (Performance standards are covered in detail later in this chapter.)

6. Dependencies and assumptions
   - List all known key dependencies relevant to the stated requirements and the potential solutions to be provided by the selected supplier. These dependencies relate to both internal (organizational) and external (economic, political, legislative, technical, market) factors.
   - Dependencies should include what the supplier requires of the customer to enable them to deliver.
   - List all assumptions made in defining the requirements and supplier deliverables. As with dependencies, they should cover the range of possible internal and external factors.

7. Constraints
   - List all known constraining factors that the supplier must adhere to and be aware of. These can include policy, organizational, budgetary, and legislative elements.
   - It can be helpful to think of restrictions, dictates, and current conditions that cannot be changed or are difficult to change.

## Scope Definition: Guidelines

The detailing of requirements at *stage four* in the template—scope definition—is the central part of the requirements document. Conciseness and clarity are key. Here are some ideas to help you achieve this.

**Focus on outputs and deliverables rather than system or process. In other words, focus on what you want to buy rather than how the supplier is to deliver it.**

This is important as the requirements definition will feed directly into the RFP. The audience for the RFP is the potential suppliers, and in the RFP, you are stating what you want them to deliver and asking them to respond with their proposed solution—the how. If the requirements definition mandates the detailed process/system, you are automatically limiting the supplier response. Stating constraints, along with assumptions and dependencies, is about providing context and relevant background—different from mandating what the solution must look like.

**Break the requirement down into several key headings. (Link back to the executive summary to check the stated need at that level.)**

A principle of effective communication is to logically structure your thinking, so that when you move from thinking to writing, the resulting document will be as easy as possible for the reader to decode and understand—in this case the readers will be internal stakeholders who will sign off the document, and ultimately, the supplier, who will be asked to respond to it. The first step is to break the requirements down into a number of key headings.

**For complex sets of requirements, break down each key heading into a number of subpoints.**

This builds on the previous point—for each key heading generate several subpoints in a logical sequencing that could, for example, be based on time, hierarchy, process steps, and so on.

**Rank requirements at the key heading level (or subheading level, if necessary) on an essential, important, and desirable scale.**

Attaching a level of priority to the requirements, or the detail points in a set of requirements, will help create focus and direction for the supplier when this is included in the RFP. In establishing these different levels there is no license for the supplier to ignore certain requirements—they must all be addressed, but in the selection criteria, demonstrating the ability to address some key requirements will have additional weighting compared with other requirements.

**For each key heading define what you are seeking to save/increase/improve/solve (SIIS model). Wherever possible, these motives and drivers should be supported with quantifiable data.**

If suppliers can understand the drivers and motives behind the stated requirements, the more focused and relevant they can make their responses in the proposals they put forward. The requirements define the *what*, the drivers and motives provide a context, as well as some insights into the *why*.

The SIIS model provides a straightforward mechanism for describing the drivers and motives. From this proposed engagement with a supplier, be it service delivery or project based, what are you seeking to *save* (money, time, resources, etc.), *improve* (accuracy, customer service, response times, final fix time, reliability, etc.), *increase* (productivity, system uptime, etc.), *solve* (specific issues and problems)?

### Define Timescales

Define timescales for the overall engagement, be it an outsourcing strategy or a specific project. The more detail provided here, the more the supplier will be able to assess what resources will be required at what points and outline their plans in the proposal.

**Define the characteristics, features, and experience that you believe a supplier must demonstrate if they are to effectively deliver what you require of them.**

While not strictly about defining requirements, establishing some initial views (at least) regarding the profile and competence of the supplier that you believe will be best able to address those requirements is useful at this stage. The conclusions will provide a feed into the RFP, where a potential supplier profile will need to be stated in detail.

## Defining Minimum Performance Levels for Key Areas

This relates to *stage five* in the template.

Closely linked to the definition of requirements is the definition of the performance levels required from a supplier in how they deliver against those requirements.

It is important to be clear about the difference between the following:

- defining the *minimum* levels of performance you would expect; minimum is a key word—it represents what is required to get through the gate and no more—and
- mandating the performance levels and the mechanisms for measuring them, generally referred to as KPIs (key performance indicators); proposing the performance levels that are possible and realistic is the responsibility of the supplier and should be included in their proposal.

If you are too prescriptive and dictate what you expect suppliers to provide, to what performance standard, along with the measurement process, then you are potentially limiting how the supplier will respond—potentially, they just play back what you stated. The problem is that far more could have been possible.

**Considering performance at the tangible and intangible levels**

To emphasize the point, at this stage we are identifying requirements and what we expect of a potential supplier, including performance levels. In terms of performance levels there are possibly two dimensions. I say *possibly*, because for some suppliers, of a more tactical nature, only level one performance requirements are necessary. For strategic suppliers, both the levels described next are invariably required.

1. Performance at the *tangible* level: These are the aspects of performance for which we can construct hard, data-based measures; for example, timeliness of delivery, responsiveness to requests, adherence to budgets, accuracy, quality, customer satisfaction (based on surveys, etc.). These are the elements that can be covered in service level agreements (SLAs) and KPIs.

2. Performance at the less tangible, *value add* items: By their very nature, they are more difficult to measure, and it is even debatable whether they should be measured in a pass/fail-type format. Examples of supplier behavior in these less tangible areas are the degree

to which process improvements are suggested: proactively, industry best practices are shared. A demonstration of interest in understanding the customer's business and strategy and how they as a supplier can support the level of (nonbillable) time invested; the degree to which they will be flexible in adapting their process to your organization, the time they will invest in understanding your culture. This thinking is important at this stage, as again it can feed into the sourcing phase and the RFP. It also helps you reflect on and define the type of relationship you want with a supplier in the context of the service delivery/project being discussed.

### Thought Provokers

1. From your experience in projects where the decision is made to provide a solution to a set of needs via an external service or project delivery, how well do you feel requirements have been defined to the required level of detail?
2. From your experience, what are the benefits of well-defined requirements, and on the other hand, the issues with poorly defined requirements?
3. From where you sit, to what extent do you feel the right people are involved in the requirements definition?
4. If it is in your sphere of responsibility (and even if it is not.), what recommendations would you make to the organization to improve how requirements are defined?

### Takeaways

From a personal learning perspective, what are your three key takeaways from this chapter?

| 1 | |
|---|---|
| 2 | |
| 3 | |

# CHAPTER 4

# Research

*In this chapter: the range of places where research fits in the lifecycle, importance and benefits of proactive research, establishing the sources of data, possible future-influencing factors, understanding the supply market, engaging with potential suppliers*

## Where Does Research Fit in the Lifecycle?

The simple answer, considering the lifecycle described in Chapter 2, is that it fits between the identification of needs and sourcing. It makes sense—you identify requirements, and before you issue the RFP to selected suppliers, you do some background research. The reason I am raising the question as to where it fits is to establish the principle that research can be and should be ongoing, sometimes as a background activity. For example, you may be in the early stages of a contract for delivery of a service, and the contract duration is three years. Does this mean that you do not continue to monitor what is happening in the marketplace, that you do not keep updated on new technologies and trends? Of course not. The ideas in this chapter are, therefore, not just set in the context of research in a specific stage of the lifecycle, but also as an ongoing activity.

There are a number of benefits of treating research as a proactive activity, rather than restricting it to a specific slot in the lifecycle. Let me give you some proof to support that statement. During many years of working with people in companies involved in the supplier lifecycle I have noticed that frequently they are under time pressure; OK, I can hear people say, "Who in a business role is not under time pressure?" Correct, but the time pressure here is quite specific—the business has identified a need, the solution is required urgently, research takes time, so the pressure is to get an RFP out as soon as possible (to the suppliers you know about and have worked with in the past), fast-track the process, get proposals in and get decisions made, engage the supplier (sometimes even before the contract is finalized). Does this sound familiar? As quoted in Chapter 2, the pressure to sell is always greater than the pressure to buy. Of course, the supplier sales teams must set their targets each month, each quarter, each year, and the canny customer knows the times during the year when the salesperson is under maximum pressure and can capitalize on it. From my aforementioned observations, however, the pressure is not always one way.

## Importance and Benefits of Proactive Research

- It takes away the potential time pressure of research having to be completed reactively as part of a supplier engagement, where there is all-too-often an urgency tag.
- It provides the opportunity to meet with suppliers on a general information exchange basis rather than on the basis of a specific project—there is more on this later in this chapter.
- It enables building a market and supplier database that can be helpful when a specific requirement is identified.
- It offers a greater the range of options, because of the information obtained, when considering the possible different solutions available, so choice is not limited.
- It gives time and opportunity to the different stakeholders involved to work collaboratively on research and fact-finding. Linking back to Chapter 2, you will recall I highlighted the risk of the lifecycle activities being treated as silos. Collaborative research is another way of avoiding this.

The previous point, opportunity for collaboration in research, raises an important question: Who has the overall responsibility for the researching stage of the lifecycle? As will become evident as you work through this chapter, there are many different activities involved, so it is very unlikely that one person or one function will pick up all the actions. The risk is, therefore, that some things get missed or that the information collected is not collated and analyzed systematically. In my experience, in most organizations there is often no obvious role/function that is responsible for all aspects of the research. In your organization, the answer may be straightforward; if not, then establishing that ownership/coordination role becomes an action point.

## Data Sources

The sources of data—where you go to find the relevant information—will vary, depending upon the products, services, or projects you have requirements for; the overall marketplace; the levels of complexity involved; and so on. There is, therefore, no one-size-fits-all generic list. What follows are two comprehensive but not exhaustive lists, categorized as either internal or external sources. As the list is generic, there is likely to be overlap of some descriptions and functions, depending on specific organizational structures.

### Internal Sources

- **Business analysts:** For any significant, complex engagement, particularly where technology is involved, it is likely that the business analyst function would have been involved in defining requirements and would have produced the detailed specifications. They are, therefore, an obvious source of data in the research stage. They can provide inputs as to how the potential solutions in the marketplace can address the requirements agreed upon.
- **Subject Matter Experts (SMEs):** These are the functional experts in relation to the service/project being outsourced—be it IT, HR, logistics, facilities management, contact centers. The SMEs are specialists in their field and will have knowledge of the supply market.
- **User groups:** They are a key group as they comprise the customers of the service. As such, they will have practical, in-depth knowledge of the requirements, will have experienced what works well and not so well with current solutions. From previous experience they may have valuable knowledge about suppliers, the marketplace in general.

- **Finance:** Money always has a part to play in any business decision. Finance can provide information on current costs, budgets for new initiatives, and of course, any financial constraints.
- **Sourcing** (procurement, purchasing—whatever the label is in your organization): Of course, they have the key role in the sourcing stage, but should also be involved in research regarding the latest thinking about types of contract, engagement methods; key suppliers in the market, their strengths and weaknesses; overall trends in procurement thinking; and so on.
- **Legal, risk, compliance:** Putting these three key functions in one heading is not meant to minimize their importance. They are responsible for ensuring that all regulatory and legal requirements are met; also, that due diligence is comprehensively carried out. These tasks are part of the sourcing/contracting function, but it is wise to involve them early on, as part of research, so that there are no surprises regarding the *legal duties and requirements* later in the lifecycle.

### External Sources

- **Current suppliers:** Current suppliers in the same/similar service area as the one you are currently seeking to source a supplier for can be an invaluable source of data. If you have developed a positive working relationship that is deeper than just the transactional level, then there should be a preparedness to share information regarding best practices, what the latest developments are in the marketplace, what new technologies are on the horizon. Of course, there must be a reality check here—a supplier will not be prepared to promote their nearest competitors, and with their business hats on, they will be tempted to engineer their responses to favor their specific strengths in relation to their competitors. Nonetheless, current suppliers are a very powerful data source.
- **Potential suppliers:** A key part of researching the market and the potential solutions to addressing the requirements is engaging with potential suppliers. How this is done and how such discussions are positioned with the supplier are very important in terms of

managing their expectations, and in some cases, not contravening any procurement regulations, which is especially relevant for public sector organizations. This area is covered in more detail later in this chapter.

- **Professional bodies and associations:** Considering your profession and role in the organization which professional associations are you a member of? Your colleagues, other stakeholders who are involved in this project, which professional bodies are they members of? Your organization, which trade associations and memberships does it have? All such membership associations can provide a wealth of information via articles, posts on LinkedIn, their own portals, and so on. What's more, much of the information is free. Ask yourself the question, to what extent am I (and colleagues) utilizing the available information from these sources?
- **Seminars and exhibitions:** There is a balance required here, as it is possible to become a professional exhibition/seminar attendee. Being selective about which ones to attend and being clear about your objectives in investing the time and the money will help create that focus. In addition to data gathering, they provide the other obvious benefit of networking with people in similar roles with similar challenges.
- **Competitors:** Possibly linked to membership of trade bodies and associations, your competitors can be a source of data, with the obvious proviso that there are limits to what information would be shared.
- **Internet:** It so obvious, it goes without saying, but for completeness I feel it must go on the data sources list—your own Internet research.

## Considering Future-Influencing Factors

Collecting information about the possible solution to a set of requirements that have been defined is complex. One of the challenges is to make some initial decisions about a solution that is required for, say, a three- or five-year period on the basis of a statement of requirements today. What might change over the period of the service delivery?

Of course, we cannot be 100 percent accurate forecasters, but we can carry out some future-proofing insurance by asking the following questions in the course of the research stage. In broad terms, there are seven categories of external factors at a generic, key heading level. More specific categories/or subheadings could apply to specific supply markets.

**Changing (external) customer needs:** Not to be confused with the requirements of the internal customer (whose requirements are the reason a supplier is being engaged), this is about how the organization's customers' requirements may change over time, and how those changes may influence what the solution for the internal customer needs to cover. *For example, if the end customer is likely to demand faster and more flexible delivery times in the mid term, then the solution for a new sales order processing and shipment system should have such capabilities built in.*

**Technology change/development:** Obviously, this is a key consideration for IT requirements and solutions; however, advances in technology impact a lot more requirements and solutions than those directly IT related. *For example, rapid advancements in artificial intelligence will undoubtedly influence requirements and solutions in the manufacturing divisions of many organizations.*

**Developments in the supply market:** What is likely to change in the supply market relevant to the requirements you are currently seeking solutions for? How could envisaged developments influence how you approach a supplier engagement? *For example, if the research suggests that in the next two to three years there are likely to be more entrants to the market, with innovative solutions, this would mean that you check with any potential supplier what their planned developments are; it may also influence the length of contract you are prepared to sign up for.*

**Regulatory demands—national, international:** What regulations is the supply market you are researching currently subject to? Will the level of regulation increase or decrease? How could these factors influence any purchasing decisions? *For example, if there is a strong possibility that regulatory frameworks will become more rigorous, it would be wise to check any potential suppliers' intent and capability to comply.*

**Demographic considerations:** These involve the degree to which demographic change could influence the requirements of your end customers and how those changes would impact the solutions you are about to consider from potential suppliers. *For example, if there is a demographic shift to a greater proportion of 50+ year-old people in the population, and they are potentially significant purchasers of your products, how could this influence the systems and processes that support your (outsourced) contact centers?*

**Cultural:** In researching the market and potential suppliers, clearly, competence is a key consideration; however, culture and cultural fit can be as important, particularly, in terms of how the future relationship can look and work. Considering the culture of your organization, and that of potential suppliers, the degree of fit is a possible factor in any subsequent decision about a supplier. This becomes a more complex question when offshoring is a potential option. *For example, if a possible option is to consider IT infrastructure development suppliers based in Asia, what are the cultural implications to think about?*

**Socioeconomic factors:** These involve the degree to which the broad economic landscape and its possible impacts on society may influence any decisions you make regarding solutions or the supplier. *For example, if there are indications that the economy will grow strongly and that incomes will increase at the same rate, then it is possible that end customers will look for additional functionality, which they will have the means to pay for, from the products/services you sell them to them, using supplier-sourced fulfillment service. This would lead you to check if the supplier systems can be functionally enhanced without any major redesign.*

By using the range of internal and external data sources listed in this chapter it will be possible to collect information across these seven factors. The exercise is about building an overall picture from which reasoned decisions can be made. It is not realistic to achieve 100 percent definitive factual data all the time, so some judgment calls will be necessary.

## Supply Market Positioning

This element of the research stage in the lifecycle is concerned with categorizing the supply market for the services you require, considering the identified needs. How the supply market is categorized and the characteristics of that category will influence the sourcing approach, and subsequently, the type of relationship with suppliers. It is important to emphasize that at this stage we are seeking to categorize the market and not specific suppliers within it. Why is it important to do this? It will provide guidance in relation to the following:

- Defining the overall sourcing approach—steps, timescales, stakeholders, decision criteria, and so on
- Making a decision about how much time and resources will be invested into the engagement—as a general rule, the more strategic, the more mission critical the service, the more time and resources allocated
- Establishing the degree of governance process that is required—legal will define what governance is required for any supplier engagement; again, there is a general rule that the more mission critical, the more strategic the service, the greater the level of governance
- Deciding the contracting model for the engagement—generally the sourcing team will be the people who can best align the service to the most suitable contracting method
- Establishing how the selected supplier will be potentially segmented—this in turn will influence how the supplier is managed; I use the term *potentially* here, as it is possible that a supplier is providing a range of services to a customer, with each of the services being categorized differently

Some points when using the model:

- It is a guide not a straitjacket.
- Different stakeholders may have different views on the supply market positioning—this is understandable and is fine. It provides a structured discussion for arriving at a considered approach to the engagement.

# The Category Portfolio Analysis: A Supply Market Positioning Model

This model was developed by Value Dynamics (2007) Ltd., which itself was developed from the original theory of Peter Kraljik, and has the following elements:

**Vertical axis:** There are several factors here that be described under the following headings, which can be summarized as *significance/ impact*. The factors are business implication, customer implication, market dynamics, ease of switching degree of lock in, and reputational implication.

**Horizontal axis:** significance of spend (based on percentage of total spend within a defined area); this could be spend in a functional area, total IT spend, total spend on a specific range of services, for example, marketing. You select the most appropriate *universe* figure to make the most sensible analysis.

The descriptors in each quadrant define the possible main drivers and strategies the customer organization may have in approaching a supply market in a category (Figure 4.1).

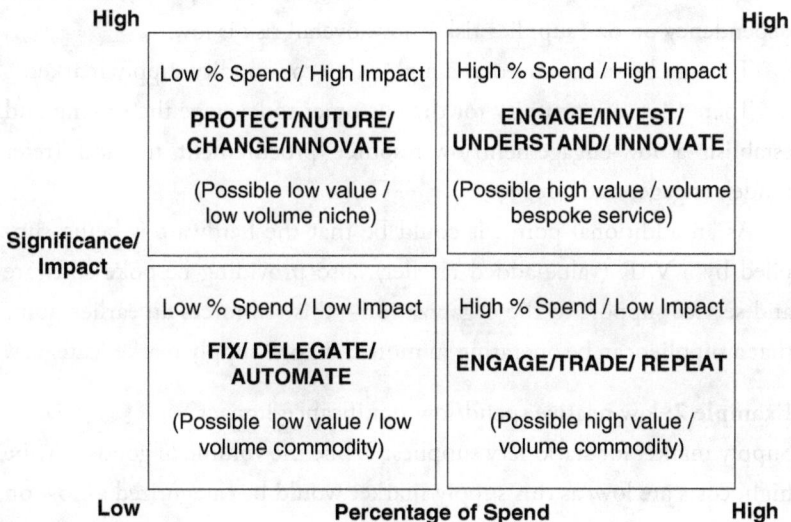

*Figure 4.1 Supply market positioning*

The model is practical, can be used to give structure to debate and discussion, and to arrive at some conclusions. To reaffirm, the objective is to define the category of the market you are working in for a specific supplier engagement, so that you can decide how you will approach the procurement. To repeat, this exercise is looking at the supply market, not a specific supplier operating within it Later on in the lifecycle the categorization can be applied to a selected supplier to help define the type of commercial relationship you want with them—remembering that a supplier could be supplying a range of services to a customer, each one falling into a different supply market category.

To help you apply the model back in your organization, I have provided some examples. I emphasize that they are *examples* only. One organization may see a supply market as highly strategic for them; another may view the same supply market as very transactional.

**Example 1:** high relative spend/low significance/impact
Supply market for laptop computers: As virtually anyone in a business/administrative function in an organization has a laptop, it is reasonable to assume that laptops purchases are sizeable and ongoing in many organizations. For the purpose of this example, we will assume that hardware spend is a significant element in the overall IT budget.

If we look at the vertical axis, there a number of suppliers; lock into/dependency on one supplier risk is low, overall risk is low.

This can be summarized as a high-value commodity supply market.

There is an opportunity for the customer to leverage the pricing and establish a low-engagement/low-resource procurement method (refer model: engage, trade, repeat).

As an additional point, it could be that the hardware is being supplied by a VAR (value-added reseller), also providing bespoke software and service support to the organization—this reinforces an earlier point that a supplier can be operating in more than one supply market category.

**Example 2:** low relative spend/low significance/impact
Supply market for stationery supplies: While the volume of goods may be high, costs are low, as this supply market would be categorized as low on spend percentage.

On the vertical axis, stationary is in the low-significance/impact category, many different suppliers, lock-in risk is low.

This can be summarized as a low-value commodity supply market.

There is an opportunity for the customer to streamline and automate the procurement process, with low time investment.

This is a typical transactional supplier–customer relationship.

**Example 3:** low relative spend/high-significance impact
Supply market for support of legacy system: Spend is relatively insignificant in the context of the overall IT support budget, but as part of the overall inventory control process, the system is crucial to the logistics and production departments.

On the vertical axis this is in the high-significance/impact category, and because of its legacy nature, there is only one viable supplier, with one other potential supplier that could pick up the support but requiring some upskilling before they could offer ongoing support. So, lock in is high, ability to move suppliers low.

This can be summarized as a low-volume niche, potentially sole-source supply market.

For the customer, the objective in the short term is to nurture and protect security of supply, with a mid-term goal of designing out and implementing a new integrated inventory control system.

**Example 4:** high relative spend/high impact
Supply market for integrated warehousing and logistics service for high-volume producers of high-value consumer goods:

This is a high-spend supply market where suppliers are delivering mission critical services to the manufacturing division of a business, which operates on a just in time (JIT) basis.

While there are a number of suppliers in this supply market, the relationship is strategic, which needs to be developed over time, as the supplier service becomes an integral part of the customer process and operations, and thus, becomes a bespoke service.

This calls for a holistic approach, where there is a preparedness and mutual benefit in understanding each other's business and working collaboratively.

## Engaging with Potential Suppliers

The potential suppliers are a prime source of data, helping to build your overall knowledge of the market and the potential solutions.

Any request for information will involve them in some work, and you need to be clear as to why you want the information and the level of information you require.

It is important that you make it clear from the outset that you are not engaging in a tendering process at this stage. There are some important reasons for this:

- If your organization is in the public sector and you go to a supplier asking for information, it could be perceived that you are entering a formal process—for example, in the United Kingdom the term often used is PQQ (prequalification questionnaire). The problem is that once a formal process is triggered, there are a set of rules about how the tender must be conducted; those rules could, for example, limit your ability to change or fine-tune the requirements and your freedom to have informal discussions with suppliers. The specific rules will depend on which country you are operating in, but the fact is that for developed economies, where there tends to be rule-based procedures, those potential constraints are present. Hence, the importance of being clear with suppliers about what the discussions are about and not about. Remove any possibility of confusion or misunderstandings.
- You need to manage the supplier's expectations. If they feel that they are being *used* to provide you with information (possibly to fulfill your requirement to get, for example, three suppliers involved in a bid), then they may feel negative. Honesty is always the best policy. Make it clear that now you are information gathering, to understand the marketplace and the suppliers within it. Suggesting that the discussions could progress to a formal request for proposal (RFP) is fine, but do not overpromise. If your organization gets the reputation of using suppliers' resources and time, with little chance of them ever securing any business, you will find suppliers will be reluctant to engage when you have a genuine need for them. Supply markets have their grapevines.

- If, on the other hand, they understand that there is no immediate piece of work involved, but that you want to be proactive in understanding what their capabilities are for future reference, they will see this as a positive, long-term selling opportunity. Hence, the importance of how you position the discussions.

In these initial discussions it is important to strike a balance between increasing your overall knowledge of the supply market and avoiding an information overload. Also, consider the supplier: How much information will they be prepared to give? How much time to invest in a speculative discussion? The following is a useful checklist.

### What Information Will You Require from Them?

This initial information gathering exercise could be completed remotely, without the need for face-to-face meetings—it depends on the context, the level of existing relationship, significance of the possible tender for you and them.

*Company background*
- Company name, address, telephone, e-mail, website details
- Parent company details
- Years of trading
- Recruitment policies
- Number of employees, broken down by function
- Summary of current/previous year turnover/profit

*Products and services*
- Summary of products /services offered
- Example(s) of clients in a similar sector/requirement
- Supporting information regarding concepts, processes, methods
- Costing structure, methodology
- Description of any subcontract/partner arrangements
- With your summary of requirements, how they see they can address them (at a concept level)

*The qualitative factors*
- Description of values, culture
- What they see as their key differentiators

## Meeting with Potential Suppliers

The most effective way of evaluating a potential supplier is to have a meeting. In this way, you can verify the information you have already gained by asking them the questions in the aforementioned checklist. In addition, a meeting provides the chance to get to know what they are like as people and gain some insights as to how the working relationship could look. Meetings take time, however, so the following can be a guide:

1. Arrange to meet the initially screened in potential suppliers where the service they can provide is significant and critical to the organization. Refer to the supply market positioning model. Invest most time in the mission critical category.
2. Have a clear agenda—an opportunity for them to build on the information they have already provided, an opportunity for you to further evaluate, and a two-way information exchange.
3. As part of the meeting, agree on the future contact plan—it will be important to manage expectations. Clarify, specifically, that at this stage the meeting or subsequent discussions are not linked to a specific opportunity or tender.

## Evaluating Potential Suppliers

You will recall that in Chapter 2, when the lifecycle was introduced, I said that while at first sight it looks like a linear process, in reality, there are not always fixed lines between the stages and at times it is an iterative process. I raise this now as a timely reminder. We are still in the research stage, so evaluation of potential suppliers is very much at an initial level. Subsequently, when the lifecycle progresses to sourcing, more detailed evaluations of suppliers will take place, measured against a set of criteria.

After receiving responses from your questionnaire, having met the screened in potential suppliers, you will be able to more accurately evaluate them—building on your initial assessment. Applying the following model provides a top-level picture of a supplier's capabilities and enables you to compare suppliers' relative strengths.

**USP**—a unique selling point, a characteristic that only they have that gives them a differentiator

**Plus factor**—not unique, but their capability/solution is better than that of competitors.

**Look alike**—their capability is the same as that of the others

**Negative factor**—their capability is inferior to that of the others

## Research Stage Checklist

There are many elements in the research stage, so here is a reminder checklist:

- Remember the significant benefits to proactively researching the market, rather than waiting for a live project or procurement.
- Use the number of internal and external sources of data that are available
- Consider the range of future-influencing factors—technology, supply market, changing needs, socioeconomic, and cultural.
- Apply the supply market positioning analysis which is a key input in deciding the engagement strategy.
- Engage with potential suppliers on an open discussion/information sharing basis, to gain an overview of their products, services, and overall capabilities.
- Evaluate the outputs from supplier meetings to establish their key strengths and carry out an objective competitive analysis.

### Thought Provokers

1. To what extent is proactive research carried out as part of the supplier engagement process in your organization?
2. On the basis of your knowledge of the organization, and how the overall supplier lifecycle operates, who/which function has the

overall responsibility for organizing and coordinating the research stage?

3. Assume you have identified who should be picking up the research coordination role; what would be the five key messages you would use to sell the idea to them?

4. What would be the biggest obstacle to introducing the research stage as part of the standard supplier engagement process in your organization? How could you overcome it?

### Takeaways

From a personal learning perspective, what are your three key takeaways from this chapter?

| | |
|---|---|
| 1 | |
| 2 | |
| 3 | |

# CHAPTER 5

# Sourcing Overview

*In this chapter: positioning this overview, different sourcing engagement models, RFI structure and content, supplier selection criteria*

## Positioning This Overview

This is not a book detailing the supplier procurement process; however, it is a key stage of the lifecycle and so is covered in this chapter, as part of the holistic supplier engagement and management journey. I do emphasize that it is at an overview level. I describe the key elements of sourcing, in generic terms; there are several different contracting models, some of which I list for reference, but the steps I describe are relevant regardless of the specific model or models used in your organization. The steps cover the different documents you need to send out to the potential suppliers requesting information regarding their proposals. The overview also covers how you approach the supplier selection task.

Depending on the time and resources available, you may have already contacted suppliers during the research stage of the lifecycle, which was covered in Chapter 4. The difference between the dialogue with suppliers in the research and sourcing phase is significant. In research, the information exchange is at a background level, with no live project/specific set of requirements being involved. In the sourcing phase, the dialogue is very specific and is about specifying needs in detail, receiving proposals to address those needs, evaluating the responses, and making decisions.

# Different Sourcing Approaches: The Relationship and Contracting Models

One of the key determinants of the approach to sourcing a supplier will be the significance of the service being outsourced to the supplier in terms of spend and overall business impact. The supply positioning model in Chapter 4 provides an explanation of how different supply markets are categorized. The output from that analysis is carried through to the sourcing phase and guides the decision in the following way:

- High value/high significance—*strategic supplier*—significant selection and appointment activity
- Low value/low significance—*transactional/commodity supplier*—relatively less selection and appointment activity

## Different Relationship Models

*Strategic* and *transactional* represent the extremes of a spectrum, and within that range, there are a number of possible contract relationship models. It is possible that one supplier could be involved with a customer on a range of engagements, each one with a different relationship model. For example, an IT supplier could be involved in an ongoing service delivery contract and in many infrastructure development projects.

The following are examples of different relationship models:

- **Partnership:** This is a very close commercial relationship, whereby customer and supplier agree to combine as one entity for a function/activity. The term has become overused, but this is the pure definition
- **Joint venture:** In a sense, this is very close to partnership, as it involves shared working on a single activity/project, but in legal terms, they are different structures.
- **Conventional fixed-term contract:** Typically, this is a three-year contract, possibly with a two-year extension at the end of the initial term, suitable for delivery of services where a degree of integration and knowledge of the customer business is required.

- **Project-based contract:** This is meant for short- to medium-term engagements, where the contract deliverables and timelines are directly driven by the project goals and milestones.
- **Framework contract:** This arrangement is convenient if there are a small number of suppliers who can, in broad terms, all provide the same type of services and there is frequent demand for that range of services in the organization. The framework involves setting up a live formal contract with each supplier; the organization then can contract with any of the suppliers within the framework without going through a full tender process that involves full a legal, risk, due diligence procedure. All that is needed is a set of requirements that any of the suppliers in the framework can quote for. In essence, frameworks save time, at the same time as providing choice and an element of competitive tendering.
- **Outsource:** The provision of a total business function is transferred out of the customer organization, to be managed, fulfilled and reported by the supplier.
- **Offshore:** As outsource, but the supplier is based in a geography different than that of the customer.

### Different Costing Models

At the next level there are different costing types/models that define the structure and mechanics for how costs, and therefore, billings are calculated for the provision of the services by the supplier.

- **Firm fixed price:** Fixed price is favored by most organizations because the price is set and is not subject to change unless the scope of work changes. Any cost increases due to adverse performance would be the responsibility of the supplier.
- **Fixed price incentive fee:** This type of contract gives the customer and the supplier some flexibility in that it allows for deviation from performance, with a financial incentive for achieving certain metrics. Generally, the incentives are related to cost, schedule, or the technical performance of the supplier. A price ceiling is set, and any costs above that ceiling are the responsibility of the supplier.

- **Fixed price with economic price adjustment:** These contracts are used for long-term engagements and allow for predefined adjustments to the contract price due to changed conditions. These could include inflation rate changes or increased or decreased costs for specific commodities.
- **Cost plus fixed fee:** In these contracts the supplier is reimbursed for allowable costs for performing the work and receives a fixed fee payment that is calculated as a percentage of the initial estimated project costs.
- **Cost plus incentive fee:** The supplier is reimbursed for allowable costs and receives an incentive fee on the basis of achieving certain performance objectives.
- **Cost plus award fee:** In these contracts the seller is reimbursed for allowable costs. The majority of the fee is earned on the basis of satisfaction of identified broad subjective performance criteria.
- **Time plus materials:** Time and material contracts are open ended in the sense that there is no fixed price at the outset, usually because a definitive statement of work was not possible.

My advice is to consult with the procurement specialists and the SMEs (for the product/service in question) as between them they will have the knowledge to advise on the most appropriate approach in the context of the best procurement practice and specific supply market knowledge.

To return to the focus for this chapter—regardless of the scale and complexity, regardless of the selected approach and contracting type—we need information from the selected suppliers, we need to analyze the information, and we need to make a decision. These tasks are covered in the rest of this chapter.

## The Key Steps in the Sourcing Process

While labels may change, when needs have been defined and potential suppliers identified, the most common approach is based on the following:

- Issuing an RFI (request for information)
- Assessing initial responses and filtering in/out

- Issuing an RFP (request for proposal)to filtered in suppliers
- Assessing responses using predefined criteria, meeting suppliers
- Making the initial decision and moving through to the next lifecycle stage

The terms RFI and RFP are generic, and widely understood. Other terms are, however, used. For example, with a specific UK reference, the public sector uses PQQ (prequalification questionnaire) instead of RFI. Not geographic specific, some organizations use ITT (invitation to tender) instead of RFP.

### RFI and RFP: Definitions

Request for Information

The RFI is the document issued to potential suppliers and performs the following functions:

1. Describes in overview terms the products/services that are required
2. Asks the supplier a range of initial questions about their ability to provide the required products/services
3. Asks the supplier if they would like to be considered for inclusion in the RFP process
4. Helps in the short-listing of suppliers on the basis of their response

Request for Proposal

The RFP is issued to potential suppliers who have passed the short listing. It performs the following functions:

1. Provides the supplier with a structured statement of requirements
2. States the information required to enable the supplier to provide a comprehensive response. This includes, for example, constraints, dependencies, and other information that provides a context for the requirements and potential solutions.
3. Provides a clear set of instructions as to the format of the required response

4. Defines the stages and timescales
5. States the commercial requirements
6. Enables responses to be compared and evaluated in objective terms

The issuing of an RFI is a clear signal to suppliers you have been talking with informally during the research phase that you are now moving to a formal tendering process.

## RFI Structure Guide

1. Introduction
    1.1 Business overview—brief history, objectives, and organization
    1.2 Project overview—objectives, key steps, and timelines
2. Requirements
    2.1 High-level statement of key requirements
    2.2 Overview of considerations
    2.3 Description of constraints
3. Instructions to suppliers
    3.1 Information required—content and level
    3.2 Timescales for response

Typical information requested in an RFI is as follows. This list links directly to point 3.1 of the aforementioned RFI structure guide:

- Company name, address, telephone, e-mail, website details
- Parent company details
- Person responsible for responding to the RFI, and future key contact
- Years of trading
- Locations
- Number of employees, broken down by function
- Summary of current/previous year turnover/profit
- Summary of products/services offered
- Brief example(s) of clients in a similar industry with similar requirements
- Supporting information regarding concepts, processes, methods, tools, and so on

- Costing structure
- Costing guideline—if possible, considering the information given in the requirements
- Description of any subcontract/partner arrangements
- Initial thoughts on how they would approach this project, and where they see their key differentiators
- Description of values, culture

**Note:** At this stage you are not looking for detail, and you are not asking the potential supplier to create a full, time consuming proposal.

### RFP Structure Guide

While the RFI should be short and concise, the RFP is comprehensive and detailed.

1. Introduction and statement of requirements
   1.1 Business overview—organization, marketplace strategy
   1.2 Project objectives, including how they link to the business goals
   1.3 Statement of requirements and supporting data
   1.4 Evaluation/selection criteria
2. Instructions to complete the RFP
   2.1 Terms of Participation—For example ageing to a NDA (nondisclosure agreement)
   2.2 Proposal due date and timetable
   2.3 Suppliers' questions
   2.4 Confidentiality
   2.5 Communications
   2.6 Contacts/account manager
   2.7 Duration and applicability of prices
3. Required response format/information
   3.1 Summary of proposed solution
   3.2 Why this solution—what else was considered
   3.3 Detailed explanation—how requirements will be addressed
   3.4 Summary of risks considered and management strategies
   3.5 Summary of key benefits of the proposed approach

4. Service Details
   4.1  Reporting overview
   4.2  Service management SLA and KPI proposition
   4.3  Escalation process
   4.4  Reward and penalty proposals
5. Pricing and Cost Structure
   5.1  Price proposal
   5.2  Pricing/costing assumptions
6. Commercial requirements
   6.1  Background information—company trading information
   6.2  Declaration of interests
   6.3  Quality assurance, accreditations
   6.4  Insurance
   6.5  Client portfolio, references
   6.6  Continuity of service planning
   6.7  Contractual requirements

### Getting the Balance Right in the RFP

The RFP is a crucial document—the clarity, conciseness, and detail will determine the accuracy and quality of supplier responses, and it is those responses that will guide to the short listing and final decision.

What do I mean by balance? If the RFP is not specific, if the description of requirements is open to interpretation, if the questions you ask are not clear, if the instructions for how the answers are to be formatted are not clear, then what you receive may not be clear. It could be based on incorrect supplier assumptions, and it might be difficult to compare like with like when all proposals are received.

Is there a risk, however, in being overprescriptive? If the parameters you set for response are too narrow, then you risk just getting a playback of what the supplier feels you want them to say. If you are mandating performance levels (rather than suggesting minimum performance expectations), then you limit the supplier thinking through what they could actually achieve, which could be better than your mandate. Of course, you must be very clear about requirements, but be open to the possible different solutions. Enable the supplier to be creative, enable them to demonstrate their experience and competence. Use their knowledge and experience.

The skill is to achieve a balance.

*There are risks in being too prescriptive:*
- Constrains supplier thinking
- You only get responses to a solution you see
- Miss out on gaining benefits of supplier experience
- You are doing all the work
- Some suppliers could see the approach as being negative

*There are risks in being too general:*
- Supplier does not get enough direction
- Statement of needs unclear
- Lack of commonality (format, detail) in responses
- Difficult to compare like for like
- Suppliers may feel that you do not know what you want and are using them to refine your thinking

## Selection Criteria and Questions Generator

You have received the responses to the RFP, these have been analyzed, and typically, suppliers will be invited to meet the decision-making group so that the proposal can be discussed in detail, specific points clarified. Also, the meeting is an opportunity to meet the people, which will provide additional insights and inputs to the decision-making process.

Having clearly defined selection criteria is key—they need to be set out in the RFP so that the supplier is clear as to how their proposal is going to be evaluated, and of course, without such criteria an objective supplier selection decision is not possible.

### Checklist for Defining the Selection Criteria

- Go back to the needs/requirements—the selection criteria must link back to these, as selection is about assessing the supplier's ability to address them.

- Refer to the required performance standards you have highlighted in the needs definition—this will ensure that your selection criteria are focused on priorities.
- Do not build a big list of selection criteria—there is no set rule, but as a guide, five to eight key criteria. Focus on what is important.
- For each criterion, list a series of questions you need answers to, as these will be the basis on which you score.
- Be clear about how you are going to make the decision—what is going to be the information source.
- Weight each of the criteria so that the relative importance of each is clear—for example, attach a percentage ranking to each.
- Qualitative criteria can be as important as a quantifiable ones—for example, company culture and behavior can be as important as industry experience.

### Selection Criteria Examples

- Presence in their marketplace—for example, must be in the top five suppliers
- Demonstration of five years' success in delivering similar projects/services
- Geographic presence—do they have resources in all areas where you have a requirement?
- Scalability—are they able to handle increases in demand of up to 50 percent in the next two years?
- Staff experience and qualifications
- Ability and willingness to work in partnership with other suppliers

### Examples of Information/Data Sources

- Public domain—company reports, accounts, credit ratings, news media
- Current client case studies
- Current client site visits
- How they have responded/behaved during the RFI/RFP process
- Quality of the RFP response—presentation, accuracy
- Information provided in the RFP response
- Their approach, style, behavior in meetings

### Question Generators

The following example questions can help you to focus on getting the necessary information to enable you to assess a supplier against your selection criteria. This is a generic list that you can add into, modify, delete— like all such checklists, treat it as a guide, not a straitjacket. The purpose is to stimulate the thought process regarding what information you need to enable you to make the correct selection decision. I appreciate that we do not live in a perfect world, and it might not be possible to get 100 percent definitive answers to all of your questions. If there are too many information gaps, this may raise some red flags; if those flags are serious, it is wise to go back to the potential supplier, request a further meeting, and ask for more data. Generally, you will need to balance data, intuition, and judgment to make the decision.

As a base rule, the more of the *right* questions you ask, the greater your chance of getting the *right* information, and the greater your chance of making the *right* decision.

### The Thought Generator Questions

*Questions and guidance notes*
  1. Are they a significant *player* in their marketplace? *Ask yourself if they need to be significant? Sometimes a smaller niche player could be more suitable.*
  2. What is their financial performance? *It is standard practice for suppliers to be asked to supply three years of annual accounts as part of their RFP response.*
  3. What experience do they have in managing contracts of a similar size/type? *In RFP, ask them to supply relevant case studies. Talking directly to current clients is recommended.*
  4. Are they in the right location(s)? You should check if physical location is relevant and important. *Is it important that they are close to you? Or should the question be "Are they close to a good supply of qualified people?"*
  5. Can they demonstrate high levels of performance in current contracts? *Similar to question 3, but that is about experience, this is about performance. Talk to current clients.*

6. Can they manage your contract within their current resources? *This and questions 7 and 8 are linked. You require a detailed response to these three questions for assurance on capability.*

7. If *yes* to question 6, how do they intend to structure their resources to manage the additional workload?

8. If *no* to question 6, what additional resources do they intend to put in place?

9. How do they recruit and train new staff? *The reason for this question is to assess their internal processes and systems as a quality assurance.*

10. What level of staff turnover do they experience? *Assess their staff turnover compared with industry norms. Significant difference could be a concern and link to question 9.*

11. Extent to which they subcontract? *Subcontracting is not a problem per se. It is important to know the contractual arrangements they have with third parties.*

12. What percentage of their business T/O would you represent? *Balance is important here. If the percentage is too high, is there a risk, and if only a small percentage, how important will you be to them? Could this influence the levels of service they would commit to you?*

13. What experience do they have in your market sector? *It would seem obvious that experience is an advantage—but could a new entrant have new, innovative ideas?*

14. What evidence was there that they had researched your company prior to the initial meeting? *Specific questions at the meeting will give you an insight for example—*"What do you know about our strategy and marketplace?"

15. How responsive were they to requests during the selection/bidding process? *As they are in the selling phase, they should be responsive—if not, and there are delays in responding, then a red flag.*

16. Has their tender response addressed all the key issues? *This is about checking their proposal against the stated requirements in the RFP and the structure of the response.*

17. To what extent did they *push back* and question the brief as given? *Questions are positive. A senior purchasing manager said to me once,* "I get worried when there are no questions."

18. What creativity/innovation did they demonstrate that adds additional value? *This links to the RFP not being overprescriptive—where did their response demonstrate thinking outside of the box?*

19. Does their response clearly define how they will report on performance against the key measures? *Reference their response to the RFP, about performance reporting. How detailed is the process they describe?*

20. Have they clearly described how they will internally respond to performance issues? *It is important to understand their processes; it is equally important as understanding their culture in resolving issues.*

21. How competitive is their bid price compared with your budget, and with other bid prices? *Price will always be a factor in selecting a supplier. Price does not, however, always represent the best value.*

22. In which areas are they demonstrating added value over their competitors? *This relates to question 21—consider price and added value in balance. What USPs are being demonstrated?*

23. To what extent is there a cultural fit between you and their organization? *Often, cultural fit can be as important as competence in contributing to a positive customer–supplier performance and relationship.*

24. What is their strategic direction? *Looking mid/long term, does their strategy fit with how you see your future requirements? Is it important?*

25. What are they investing on development? *This links to question 24—are their future capabilities and services going to be aligned to your needs?*

26. What are their growth plans? *To what extent do you see your requirements for their services expanding significantly in the mid/long term?*

27. What is their ability to scale up if your requirements increase? *This is similar to question 26, but more focused on their ability to upscale capacity in the immediate/short term.*

The following selection criteria and selection decision charts provide practical guides/checklists as to how to capture and analyze the information from the RFP responses and other data sources. The outputs provide a basis for discussion and rational decision making by the selection decision-making group.

*Selection criteria chart*

| Criteria | Weighting % | Information Required | Data Source |
|---|---|---|---|
| List all criteria | Apply weighting 1–10 for each criterion | Define the information required | List sources of data for each information area |

*Selection decision chart*

| Criteria/ Weighting | Supplier 1 Scores 1–10 [wt.] | Supplier 2 Scores 1–10 [wt.] | Supplier 3 Scores 1–10 [wt.] |
|---|---|---|---|
| List all criteria with agreed rating 1–10 | Apply weighted scores to supplier 1 | Apply weighted scores to supplier 2 | Apply weighted scores to supplier 3 |
| Total (weight) scores ▶ | | | |

## Thought Provokers

1. To what extent do you feel that the different possible relationship and costing models are considered as part of the sourcing stage of the lifecycle in your organization?
2. In your experience, in your current role in your organization, is the required amount of time allowed for the RFI and RFP processes to be carried out thoroughly?
3. In your view, are the RFPs issued in your organization too prescriptive, too general, or just about right?
4. To what degree do you feel that supplier selection is based on a set of objective criteria?
5. Do you feel that price and other criteria are considered in the correct balance?

## Takeaways

From a personal learning perspective, what are your three key takeaways from this chapter?

| 1 | |
|---|---|
| 2 | |
| 3 | |

# CHAPTER 6

# Contract Knowledge and Supplier Background

*In this chapter: what you need to know about the contract, overview of SLAs (service level agreement) and KPIs (key performance indicators), supplier background information, supplier and customer segmentation, how to optimize the relationship*

## Setting the Context for This Chapter

Until now the chapters have dealt with the presourcing and sourcing stages of the lifecycle; in this chapter, we move to the live supplier engagement, namely, the integrate and deliver stages of the IRSID lifecycle. Integrate represents the setup activities that take the engagement from the plan as outlined in the agreed contract to live status; integrate also includes transitioning from the current situation and method of service delivery—for example, moving from the current in-house IT support desk to the IT support outsource contract. When the transitioning actions are complete, the lifecycle moves to D, the delivery stage, which represents the new business as usual (BAU). This is when the ongoing management of the performance of and relationship with the supplier is the prime supplier management activity.

When you read *in this chapter*, you may have thought, "surely, we already know about the contract"? We have already appointed a supplier, so we have all of the background information about them? Hopefully, this is true, but the importance of this part of the integrate/transition stage is that it is where responsibilities get handed over. From your side as the customer, whereas the sourcing, legal, and risk people will have had a prime role until now, with the contracts signed and the move to live status, the delivery manager and the supplier relationship manager take over the prime role, with the previous functions moving more to the background. You will recall that when I introduced the lifecycle model in Chapter 2, I highlighted the problem of each stage in the lifecycle being treated on a stand-alone, silo basis. The more this can be made seamless, the less dramatic the handover from *plan* to *live* will be. Staying with the subject of changing functions, this is also true on the supplier side. The supplier sales team will hand over to their project management and delivery team. So it is likely that on both sides new people become involved, or at least move from a less to a more significant role.

For you on the customer side, it is vital that your people taking over the responsibility for the successful running of the contract and effective management of the supplier know the following:

- What is in the contract, what the supplier is contracted to deliver, to what standard, and how that performance is to be measured
- All relevant information about the supplier, including how they are categorized on a segmentation model, as this will determine how the relationship is to be managed and what degree of management time is to be invested in it

## What You Need to Know about the Contract

The contract is probably a very long document as it will include the full legalese text that is required in a formal, legally binding contract—what are often referred to as the *boilerplate items*. The people responsible for managing the supplier delivery will not need to be familiar with every line of the contract, but they will need to know what the supplier is contracted to deliver and to what standard—*you cannot manage a supplier's performance if you do not know what is in the contract*. This may sound odd, but from my experience in facilitating training courses on supplier management over a number of years, it is not uncommon for participants to say, "I have never seen the contract; I do not know what the key measures of performance are." The following checklist would have provided them with some guidance as to what they need to have or find out.

I suggest that this is the minimum information required; the more information you have over the minimum, the better.

Minimum contract information checklist:

- Essentially, what is the supplier contracted to deliver as a minimum in terms of the product/service, to time, to price, to quality?
- What engagement model was used, for example, is there an overriding framework contract in place with this supplier?
- Costing model—For example, fixed price, T+M (Time and materials), and so on.
- What are the agreed upon key performance measures—SLA (service level agreement), KPIs (key performance indicators), project deliverables, milestones?
- How is the performance measured, by whom, and in what report format?
- Who is the contract owner(s)?
- What is the escalation process? Penalties and incentives?
- What provisions are there for scope change and KPI refinement?
- What is built into the contract in terms of provision for exit?

## SLAs and KPIs

The SLA, a subset of the main contract, describes in detail what services the supplier is contracted to deliver, to what standard, and how the service delivery is to be managed. KPIs are a part of the SLA and describe which key aspects of performance are to be measured and how. A SLA should provide all of the information included in the following checklist—it is, therefore, vital to understand what is in the SLA if the contract is to be managed effectively.

So, to briefly recap:

- There is the main contract.
- The SLA is a part of the main contract.
- The KPIs are a subset of the SLA.

In the chapter on sourcing, I stated that there are numerous contract types and different costing models; I described a generic model. I have taken the same approach here and have taken the SLA as the generic label to describe the document that details the scope of work, performance levels, and so on. In your organization, other models and terms may be used—for example, depending on the sourcing model and contract, the SLA could be labeled as work pack; statement of work; or in the case of a project, scope and deliverables. The label does not matter; for reference I have provided here a typical SLA checklist/template.

## SLA Structure Checklist—Key Headings and Supporting Detail

1. **General/opening statement**—summary of the purpose of the SLA; preferred approach in finalizing the SLA; SLA should be seen as a living document that will form a cornerstone of the ongoing relationship

2. **Overview of the service(s) to be provided**—summary of the service to be provided; the customer/end user group(s), their needs and expectations

3. **Detailed service description**—detailed description of all aspects of the service delivery; for each element, a summary of the activities and processes involved; service level targets—the agreed and required level of performance for outputs of each element of the service delivery; responsibilities of each party; requirements/dependencies of each party

4. **Performance measurement/review**—definition of the KPIs that represent the most important outputs of activity, that need to be measured, and are selected from the service level targets; agreement that the KPIs can be amended over time as different service level targets become more/less important in the light of changing customer priorities; qualitative/value added review of performance—for example, proactivity, innovation—should also be clearly defined; frequency and format of reporting; responsibility for provision of reporting; trigger points for corrective action/escalation; any service credits/service incentive processes and methodologies

5. **Policies**—change management; business continuity; escalation and dispute resolution

6. **Contingency and planning contract end**—supplier responsibilities during contract exit; handover/transition role; transfer of information

7. **Key contacts**—supplier end—project/program managers, account manager, senior management; customer end—supplier management, procurement, customer management; first- and second-level escalation points; all operational, business, and strategic relationship owners
8. **Supplier/service delivery review**—frequency, format, medium, attendees, roles and responsibilities

## KPIs

These are an integral element of the fourth point in the SLA template. A KPI is a metric to enable you to accurately assess how the supplier is performing against a performance target. A number of performance targets will have been agreed upon as part of the contract negotiation and are included in the detailed service description, point 3 of the SLA. In theory, for each performance target there will be associated KPIs. In reality, however, it is possible that KPIs are set only for the priority performance targets. Other performance targets can still be tracked as part of overall performance reporting. The benefit of this approach is that there can be a strong focus on the top-ranked performance targets.

Knowing what the KPIs are, and how they were arrived at, is vital. Without clearly defined KPIs it is not possible to discuss performance with a supplier in a rational, objective manner. Performance review is a key part of the supplier manager role, and the forum/frequency of review will have been defined in the governance section of the contract. How these reviews are carried out is covered in detail in Chapter 11.

To ensure performance is measured objectively, KPIs need to be clear, unambiguous, and quantifiable. Designing KPIs using the SMART formula is a way of ensuring this clarity. SMART is an acronym for the following:

- Specific
- Measurable
- Ambitious
- Realistic
- Time lined

Specific, measurable, and time lined are a given for any KPI. "Ambitious" and "realistic" need to be considered in context. For example, if the discussion is around a required performance superior to the past, then the new level would be ambitious (something better) but should be balanced with achievable in the time frame (realistic).

During the course of the contract it is likely there will be the need to fine-tune or change KPIs. This is covered in detail in Chapter 11, where I will introduce you to the concept of key performance questions (KPQs). As a precursor, see the following practical checklist for how to approach the task of designing KPIs:

- Go back to the requirements, business needs as defined in the requirements document and the RFP.
- Define the *key* aspects of performance (do not try to measure everything).
- Generate the initial ideas of what the performance targets should be (use current standards, desired standards, reality check).
- Establish the obviously quantifiable elements.
- Agree how they will be measured—think SMART—and how verification will take place.

## Supplier Background Information

### The Essential Information You Need about a Supplier

Assume that you have a service delivery manager role in your organization. A new contract has recently been signed with a supplier, and you have been asked by your manager if you can take over the overall management of the relationship. This is less than ideal as a colleague was due to take on this role but they have been seconded to a project in a different area, unexpectedly. You have, therefore, had very little involvement with this supplier engagement to date. You have managed to read the RFP documents, the supplier's proposals, and an outline of the agreed contract. Your manager has called you to a meeting; the objective of the meeting is to get you briefed on the supplier background. The final comment from your manager in the invitation e-mail was "Think through the information you would like about the supplier before you meet them in a few days' time." This checklist might be helpful.

### Checklist: Information Required about All Suppliers (New/Existing)

- How significant is this supplier to the company?
- How significant is the company to the supplier?
- How significant is this initiative/project to the company?
- Examples of other clients they work with?
- What other initiatives is/could the supplier be involved in?
- What were the selection criteria for the engagement?
- What were this supplier's key strengths (compared with those of others)?
- Where did the supplier score least well (compared with others)?
- Who are the key operational and escalation contacts?

### Checklist: Additional Points for Existing Suppliers

- What has their performance been in other/previous contracts?
- Other evidence of supplier performance—customer satisfaction surveys?
- In addition to KPI measures of achievement, to what extent have they added value?
- Is there any evidence of escalations during previous work?
- What is their general attitude/responsiveness to our requests?
- What is our total expenditure with them?

If you can get answers to the aforementioned questions, you will have a good starting point.

## Supplier and Customer Segmentation

During the research/sourcing stage of the lifecycle there would have been some analysis and positioning of the supply market related to the services you wish to acquire. That initial categorization would have influenced the amount of time and the approach that was taken during the sourcing/selection stage. The segmentation of the specific supplier, now that they are engaged, is a logical part of the integration phase. How you segment a supplier and how they segment you will have a significant influence on the approach you take to managing the supplier relationship during the integration and delivery stages of the lifecycle.

As the customer you will probably have a clear idea of where you categorize the supplier in the segmentation model. You may have a view as to how the supplier views you as a customer, but it is likely that this view and understanding will develop over time.

The key is to have an understanding of segmentation models, how they are applied, and the implications. For example, from the customer perspective, are all suppliers the same? Will you invest equal time in all supplier relationships? What are the factors that will drive your decisions? From the supplier perspective, how do they view you as a customer? Do they see all customers as being equal? What are the factors that will drive their decisions?

Getting answers to these questions; gaining an insight into their perspective, how they see the world; and understanding the implications will help you establish your plan for optimizing the relationship. *Optimizing is about investing the correct amount of time to create the most value.*

We will look at two models to help in this process:

- How you categorize/segment them
- How they categorize/segment you

Before we look at the details of each, some important points about context.

- These are generic models that have been developed to provide a framework for thinking.
- There are many different segmentation models, however, and in your organization you may have developed your own processes or other generic models may have currency; in which case, it makes sense to use them.
- They can assist you in developing your thinking as to how the relationship can be optimized. I have stated earlier that any such

models are intended to be an aid and are not a straitjacket. They will help make informed decisions.

### Applying Segmentation Models

- At a corporate level a supplier will be seen in a specific segment/ category. At a specific contract/project level, however, a supplier could be seen differently—this is understandable and is not an issue as long as individual operational managers see the bigger picture. A large supplier could be providing different services to different parts of the business, and at a category/segmentation level, each one could quite legitimately be different.
- Segmentation is dynamic. Suppliers can change/influence their positioning, or you as the customer can move suppliers from one segment to another—it becomes part of the review process.
- Understanding how the supplier segments you is important as it will influence how the relationship develops. This understanding will build over time—from how they behaved in the bidding stage, how they respond to your requests, how much time they invest in you as an account (Figure 6.1).

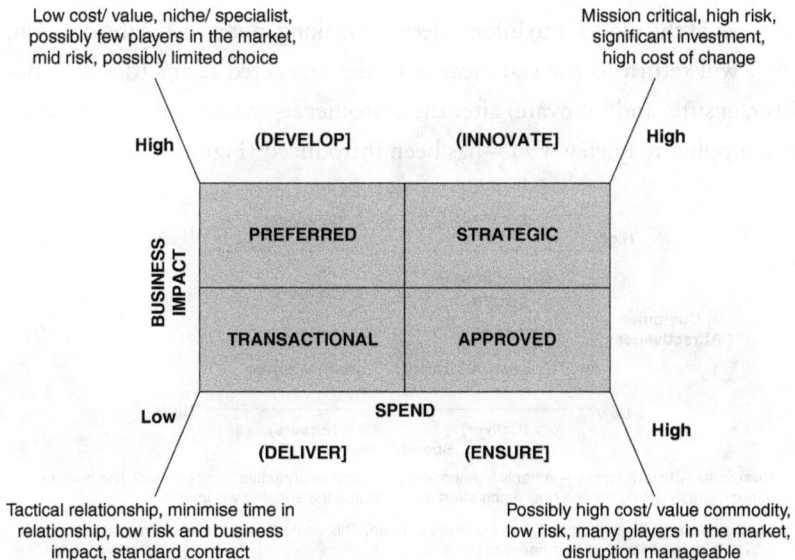

Low cost/ value, niche/ specialist, possibly few players in the market, mid risk, possibly limited choice

Mission critical, high risk, significant investment, high cost of change

| | High | (DEVELOP] | (INNOVATE] | High | |
|---|---|---|---|---|---|
| | | PREFERRED | STRATEGIC | | |
| BUSINESS IMPACT | | TRANSACTIONAL | APPROVED | | |
| | Low | SPEND | | High | |
| | | (DELIVER] | (ENSURE] | | |

Tactical relationship, minimise time in relationship, low risk and business impact, standard contract

Possibly high cost/ value commodity, low risk, many players in the market, disruption manageable

*Figure 6.1 Supplier segmentation*

### Supplier Segmentation: How You See Them

- **Business impact**—criticality of service to the business, implications of service disruption, difficulty/ease of exit, level of market difficulty (level of lock in/choice)
- **Spend**—significance of the spend involved, can be expressed in absolute or percentage terms

The *spend* dimension is reasonably straightforward. Generally, the spend with a specific supplier makes most sense viewed in the context of the overall divisional/departmental budget—for example, as a percentage of IT, HR, telecoms, marketing, or logistics budget. A central function (such as procurement) may, however, want to view spend significance with a supplier in relation to total spend with all suppliers across the business. As long as there is an agreed way of calculating this across the organization, and from this there is an agreed strategy for managing the supplier, this is the most important factor.

The *business impact* dimension is more complex, as there are a number of factors involved. More judgment calls will, therefore, be needed. For example, a supplier could score high on business impact purely on the criticality of the service they provide—even if the lock in factor is not high and the ease of exit reasonably straightforward. The level of mission criticality should be the prime factor, with the other elements being contributory to the decision. The purpose of the model is to inform decision making, not to make the decision.

I will return to the significance of the bracketed terms (develop, deliver, ensure, and innovate) after the customer segmentation model—how the supplier may view you—has been introduced (Figure 6.2).

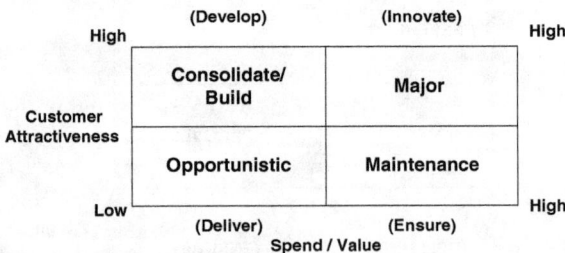

**Customer Attractiveness** – What is it that makes a customer attractive to a supplier? The level of attractiveness will determine how much effort and resource the supplier will invest.

**Spend / Value** – The volume of your business to them. This could be in absolute terms or as a % of their total sales, or compared to other clients.

*Figure 6.2 Customer segmentation*

## Customer Segmentation: How They See You

The model works on two dimensions.

### Spend / Value

This involves the volume of your business to them, in revenue terms—they may calculate this as in absolute against their total sales revenue volume or as a percentage. The calculation could be made on a division, operating country, or broader geographic basis. A supplier may also consider potential revenue—for example, a customer in the top left box may have no revenue growth opportunity for the supplier, in which case they would have a consolidate label; if there is possible revenue growth, then they may be assigned the build label, with the overall aim of moving the customer into major.

### Customer Attractiveness Factors

There are a number of other appeal or customer attractiveness factors, so as with assessing business impact in the supplier segmentation model, a degree of judgment needs to be exercised.

Possible appeal/attractiveness factors are as follows:

- Revenue opportunity
- Growth potential
- Profitability—good margin business opportunity
- Closeness of existing relationship
- Financial stability
- Strategic fit
- Early adopters—taking on new ideas?
- Level of competition—low being attractive
- Market presence
- Focused on value from suppliers rather than low prices
- Your market—is your market where they have competence and reference points?

### Mapping the Two Models

I have often been asked how the two models can be mapped and aligned, or indeed, if they are aligned. While the two models are based on different dimensions, there is a sensible correlation of common motives, on the basis of the segmentation positioning. If you go back to the two models, you will see in brackets the customer expectations and supplier motivators and drivers. The correlation can be interpreted in the following way.

*Bottom right quadrant both models:*
- Supplier in approved category—customer would expect them to ensure delivery
- Customer in maintenance category—supplier would plan to meet KPIs
- There is a correlation of the two sets of motives.

*Bottom left quadrant both models:*
- Supplier in transactional category—customer would expect them to deliver
- Customer in opportunistic category—supplier would react to a request and deliver
- There is a correlation of the two sets of motives.

*Top left quadrant both models:*
- Supplier in preferred category—customer would expect them to develop (capabilities/services)
- Customer in key development category—supplier is prepared to invest (in relationship/capabilities)
- There is a correlation of the two sets of motives.

*Top right quadrant both models:*
- Supplier in strategic category—customer would expect them to innovate
- Customer in major category—supplier is keen to demonstrate innovation
- There is a correlation of the two sets of motives.

So, at notional level, the analysis shows a similarity of expectations and drivers for customers and suppliers for the given positions in both models.

The value of the segmentation exercise is to be clear as to how you view the supplier, the service they provide, and how you intend to work with them; also, to build an understanding of how the supplier views you as a customer, so you can determine where the common goals and motives are, and as importantly, where they are not common. The greater the degree of commonality of the respective positions on the models, the greater the chance that the relationship will be based on common expectations.

At first sight this analysis may feel interesting but maybe just theoretical; however, there are some very important implications for customer–supplier relations. For example, if a customer views a supplier in the *preferred category*, they would expect the supplier to be keen to develop the relationship, but the supplier sees the customer in the maintenance category, so would aim to meet the KPIs and no more; is this going to be a satisfactory relationship? The customer will expect the supplier to invest time in the relationship, to develop their resources to provide better solutions. They will be disappointed, as the supplier will not be prepared to invest. Likewise, if a supplier sees a customer as a potential major account, but the customer sees no more than a transactional relationship, then there is a disconnect of expectations.

It is important to remember that segmentation is dynamic—both parties can move or be moved from one segment to another over time.

## Optimizing the Relationship

To recap, optimizing the relationship is about investing the correct amount of time to create the most value. The segmentation exercise will provide you with direction as to where you want to take the business relationship. In broad terms, there are three options:

- **D:** Develop—you are prepared to invest in the relationship as you believe the supplier has more to offer, and as a business you gain more value.

- **M:** Maintain—the supplier is delivering the current product service to a satisfactory level. You do not feel they can offer more, so there is no value in investing in the relationship.
- **D:** Detune—this could be because you want to eventually exit because of performance or the need for the service is diminishing or you want to de-risk by moving to more than one supplier.

Once you have defined the optimum relationship, you can establish action plans with the supplier to get there.

### Thought Provokers

1. To what extent do you feel that the essential elements of a contract are communicated to the people who have to manage the performance of a supplier in your organization?
2. Given your knowledge of supplier contracts in your organization, do you believe that typically the KPIs set out in the SLA conform to the SMART formula?
3. Is there a formal supplier segmentation model that has currency in your organization? If not, should there be?
4. How open do you feel the relationships your organization has with its key suppliers are? Open enough for the suppliers to be confident to state how you are positioned on their segmentation model?

### Takeaways

From a personal learning perspective, what are your three key takeaways from this chapter?

| 1 | |
|---|---|
| 2 | |
| 3 | |

# CHAPTER 7

# Internal Stakeholder Management

*In this chapter: internal stakeholders in the context of managing suppliers, internal stakeholder categories, seeing supplier management as a project (RACI, the INFORM model), establishing the communications network (COMNET)*

## Internal Stakeholders in the Context of Supplier Management

The lifecycle stages determine the sequence of the chapters in this book. In Chapter 6, which covered what we need to know about the contract and the supplier, I stated that we had moved to the live engagement phase of the lifecycle—integrate or the transitioning stage. So now there are two questions to answer before we get into the detail of the chapter.

First, why am I including a chapter on internal stakeholders in a book about how to manage suppliers? The reason is that people in a supplier delivery management or supplier relationship management role are often the conduit between the supplier and the end customers and other interested parties in the organization—in other words, the stakeholders. In fact, typically, the supplier management function is seen by the internal stakeholders as the supplier. The fact that the role is facing two ways—on the one hand *representing the customer to the supplier* and on the other *representing the supplier to the customer*—is fundamental to the role and the source of some of the challenges involved. The view has been put to me more than once: "Managing the supplier is relatively straightforward compared with managing the internal stakeholders." More of that later, particularly in chapter thirteen, where we discuss how change requests should be managed.

The second question to be answered is why introduce the idea of the internal stakeholder now, when we are at stage four of the five-stage lifecycle? The reason is that the focus for this chapter is to give some guidance for managing the internal stakeholders for the live engagement period of transition, through to deliver and business as usual. It is true that stakeholder engagement and management is a prerequisite for effective management of the entire supplier lifecycle, starting with stage one, identification of requirements. I stated in the introductory chapter that while the lifecycle initially looks like a straightforward, linear process, in reality it is more complex—at points it is iterative, and some activities—internal stakeholder management being one of them—are at play and active at all stages. The stakeholders may change as the lifecycle progresses; stakeholders' involvement can vary in intensity; some stakeholder functions, for logical reasons, may leave the stakeholder group, other functions may join. It is a dynamic. *The indisputable fact is that someone has to be responsible for the management of and communication across the stakeholder group.*

How am I defining a stakeholder in the context of a supplier service delivery or a supplier delivered project? In the context of suppliers and service/project delivery, *A person, team, or organization that has an interest in the supplier, the contract, the services being delivered and their impact on the business.* This is a broad definition. It highlights a key fact, however: Supplier management is more than just managing suppliers.

## Internal Stakeholder Categories

The following list provides examples of stakeholder categories, and typically, the roles and functions that could fit into those categories. These examples can and will vary depending on the service being delivered, the size, complexity, and so on.

### Examples of Stakeholder Categories and Functions in Each Category

*Contract/project owners/interfaces*
- Strategic sponsor
- Sourcing—contract owner
- Relationship management
- Service delivery management
- Transformation management
- Supply/demand management
- Project management

*Subject matter experts (SMEs)*
- Technical
- Products
- Markets

*Specialist functions/control functions*
- Legal
- Risk
- Compliance
- Finance

*Business*
- Business sponsor
- Budget holder

*User groups*
- Service/product users
- End customers

This listing can be used as a checklist for any supplier engagement for the following purposes:

- Verify that all relevant roles/functions have been identified—use this list as a base, which you can add into or delete from.

- Check that you can put names to each function or role. This is key—filling the information gaps becomes a priority action. One person may have more than one role, so a specific contact name can appear more than once.

# Using RACI

The internal stakeholder listing can feed into the building of a RACI chart. RACI is primarily a project management tool. It can be applied to the setting up and implementation of a supplier delivery management contract; in fact, often, a supplier is being engaged to deliver a project, so the transfer of the model into supplier management application is straightforward.

The RACI model is a practical tool used for identifying roles and responsibilities and thereby avoiding confusion and lack of clarity during a project. The acronym RACI stands for the following:

- **Responsible:** This relates to the person who does the work to achieve the task. They have responsibility for getting the work done or decision made. As a rule, this is one person; examples might be a business analyst, application developer, or technical architect.
- **Accountable:** This relates to the person who is accountable for the correct and thorough completion of the task. This must be one person and is often the project executive or project sponsor. The person(s) in the responsible role (described above) in a sense reports into the person(s) in the accountable role
- **Consulted:** This involves the people who provide information for the project and with whom there is a two-way communication. This is usually several people, often SMEs.
- **Informed:** These are the people kept informed of progress and with whom there is a one-way communication. They are affected by the outcome of the tasks, so need to be kept up-to-date.

Carrying out a RACI analysis enables you to add to the stakeholder information—allocating a role/responsibility. This is particularly helpful when I introduce the communications network later in this chapter.

# The INFORM Model

RACI is very definitive—it provides a guide to complete a matrix that allocates roles/responsibilities to job positions and people. It provides a map, increases understanding.

The INFORM model can be used alongside RACI. The first two elements—identify and nominate—are essentially a mirror of the analysis that RACI guides you through. In the subsequent steps, however, INFORM focuses more on the analysis of the attitudes and views the various stakeholders have. This provides very useful context, as you can build a picture of not just who the stakeholders are and their organizational role, but also about how they feel, which can provide insights into their behaviors. Are they supporters? Can they be a champion for the change/supplier? What is their influence? Might they be blockers? What might their concerns be?

Think of INFORM as providing a thought map.

The steps are as follows:

### Identify

Identify the stakeholders for your service, product, or project delivery. A stakeholder is anyone who has a vested interest in the project/initiative—someone who wants it to succeed but equally someone who doesn't. You cannot start managing stakeholders until you know who they are. Who are the main groups or departments affected by the supplier delivery or project? Suppliers—be they internal or external—are stakeholders.

### Nominate

Given the context—your operational role in the management of the engaged supplier—the stakeholders are already nominated and identified and should be known. Your task is to ensure that they are included in all communications as required. During the life of a project or service contract, stakeholders can change, so tracking and understanding those changes is part of the role.

### Find out

Analyze the attitudes of the people who have been identified as your key stakeholders—those named individuals who represent each stakeholder group. Contact them and explain about the contract, supplier, and project you are managing. Build an understanding of how they feel about the supplier, the service, or project that is being delivered. Are they supporters? Are they detractors? Are they ambivalent?

### Observe

When you have established where your key stakeholders sit, you can start to gain an understanding of their specific objectives and interests, their feelings and views on the project, the service delivery, and the supplier. Observation will also enable you to define who the supporters are, the opinion formers, and also those with reservations, and therefore the potential blockers.

### Review

Review of the stakeholders is vital. People and job roles change; so do projects and service delivery requirements. Your stakeholder list is, therefore, a dynamic—individuals and functional representatives may need to be brought in as, for example, the scope of a service contract develops; a significant stakeholder at a project kickoff may have less interest as the project evolves, so their involvement could diminish or cease. Make sure you brief any new stakeholder representative on the background, current situation, and future steps.

### Manage

The last step is to monitor and manage your stakeholders and their expectations as the project progresses or through the evolution of the service provision. Stay tuned to changing requirements of the business, and be the link between the internal stakeholders and the supplier. Involve the internal stakeholders as required in supplier reviews and use the COMNET to ensure they are fully updated.

# The Communications Network: The COMNET

After analysis using the internal stakeholder information and the RACI and INFORM models, the next and final step is to design the communications network—the COMNET.

It is a simple and straightforward tool that defines the following:

- What information needs to be communicated
- By who
- To whom
- In what format
- At what frequency

It forms the basis for stakeholder reporting requirements and takes it to an individual responsibility level. On the basis of the concept of initiators and receivers, in a communication network everyone is an initiator (sender) and/or a receiver (recipient) of information. With each initiator having a clear set of sender responsibilities, a whole stakeholder communication network is established.

As with the INFORM model, the COMNET is not a formal process—you will most likely have formal procedures in place—it is designed to give some structure to the thought process. By thinking about initiators and recipients of communication, the network can be designed and the information dropped into the formal reports (Table 7.1).

I have consciously focused on internal stakeholders in this chapter. My final point is that for the stakeholder management process to work most effectively you now need to extend the stakeholder members so that the *supplier* is included. If you recall the definition of stakeholder at the beginning of this chapter, *A person, team, or organization that has an interest in the supplier, the contract, the services being delivered and their impact on the business,"*—the supplier definitely qualifies. So, the supplier must be included in the COMNET.

*Table 7.1 COMNET template*

| Initiator: | Name: | | Role: | |
|---|---|---|---|---|
| Information | Recipient(s) | Purpose—information/ action | Format/medium | Frequency |
| | | | | |
| | | | | |
| | | | | |
| | | | | |
| | | | | |
| | | | | |
| | | | | |
| | | | | |
| | | | | |
| | | | | |
| | | | | |
| | | | | |
| | | | | |
| | | | | |
| | | | | |

## Thought Provokers

1. Who in your organization (i.e., what role/function) is responsible in a given supplier engagement for identifying the internal stakeholders?
2. To what extent do current processes for identifying stakeholders and their roles and responsibilities work effectively?
3. How do you feel stakeholder communication works in your organization? How could it be improved?

## Takeaways

From a personal learning perspective, what are your three key takeaways from this chapter?

| 1 | |
|---|---|
| 2 | |
| 3 | |

# CHAPTER 8

# Establishing the Working Code

*In this chapter: what is a working code, why it is important, considerations about how a supplier might view the idea of a working code, how to introduce it and get it agreed to, checklist of possible code statements*

## What Do We Mean by *Working Code?*

The contract clearly defines what the supplier will deliver to the customer, to what timescales, to what quality, and to what costs. So by the time we get to this point in the lifecycle—post sourcing, integrating, and moving toward deliver—there should be clarity about the *what*.

While the sourcing discussions and meetings may have covered aspects of the future relationship, in reality, in most cases the focus would have been on the tangible, hard, legal and financial elements. Relatively little time would have been spent on what we could call the *soft factors*—how the customer and supplier are going to work together.

Is it important for both parties to have a mutually understood and agreed way of working? In my view, it is crucial. No matter how well defined the requirements, how well detailed the contract, how precise the performance measures, how well the job roles and responsibilities on both sides are defined, the future will involve shifting requirements, disagreements, even disputes. If we wait for these issues to hit us, which they will, then there are two challenges: first, to overcome the substance of the issue, and second, to figure out how you are going to approach the resolution.

If there is an agreed way of working in place, encapsulated in what I call the *working code*, then when the problems arise you will know *how* to approach them.

In introducing the notion of the working code we are entering the world of culture, which is a big topic. I cover culture in more detail in the next chapter, specifically in the context of cross-cultural working. For the moment, here are some brief definitions of culture in the corporate context:

- *The way we do things around here*
- *The behavioral norms, what is accepted*
- *The way an organization communicates internally and to the outside world*
- *Behavior that is influenced by the values of the organization*

Having described the context, here is the meaning of the working code—*a set of agreed upon statements that describe mutual expectations of how we are going to behave toward each other*. Simple? Yes, the concept itself is incredibly simple, and that is its power; however, reaching an agreement on those statements as well as getting them implemented across the customer and supplier teams takes some thought and planning.

## Some Questions, Thoughts, and Observations

### Is It Not Just a Question of Sharing Each Other's Vision and Value Statements?

There are a couple of points here. First, if there are two sets of corporate vision and value statements that genuinely have currency and are applied by employees in both organizations, then this is a great starting point. Implementing any initiative in any organization is always easier if driven from the top down. However—and I stress that this is a reality check and not a defeatist statement—how many of those grand statements are really lived at the operational level in organizations? There are organizations that are an exception, but generally the statements just stay on the website or form the text for glossy PR brochures. The answer, therefore: Use the corporate-level statements if they have meaning, but the working code is best implemented at the operational team's level, between the customer and supplier teams working on the specific project or service delivery.

### It Sounds Very Theoretical and Soft: Will Suppliers Really Buy Into It?

It is interesting to take the question back a step and ask if the supplier management function in the customer organization sees it as being theoretical and impractical. With any new idea, questions and even some skepticism are inevitable; in many ways this is positive, as long as there is an openness to listen and be influenced by a sound argument. During my years in facilitating training seminars on supplier management, and this topic in particular, I have experienced many discussions. For a period of time I was working with a major investment bank that employed external suppliers for a range of services including IT, facilities management, and back office processes. Now, I state this with no negative sense, that the investment banking sector is known for taking a rational, bottom-line focused approach to business. I recall discussions with some of the supplier delivery managers about the merits or otherwise of proposing a joint working code with key suppliers. They were not sure; I suggested they tried it on a sample basis, and over a period of time, I won some converts. A key reason for the conversion was I was able to point out that they were doing this because there is a bottom line, tangible business benefit as well as a more positive and collaborative relationship. To recall a statement made in Chapter 2: *There is a clear link between a positive relationship and good performance.* So, to return to the question, will suppliers buy into it? My view is that if you, in the supplier management function, buy into it, then the suppliers will be influenced positively. There are real benefits for both parties.

### How Formal Should We Make It? Should It Be a Part of the Contract?

Balance is needed here. In a sense the working code could be described as an *emotional contract*, as it is an agreement about a set of behaviors; it is describing a working culture. If it becomes a part of the legal contract, the risk is that it will be seen as a condition, another part of process, resulting in it losing its meaning and power. On the other hand, if it is mentioned once at a meeting and verbally agreed upon with no other record, then the risk is that it has no focus and stays as a good idea. It is possible to document what has been agreed upon, so that there is a record and a reminder, without making it formal in the contract sense. If the agreed upon behaviors are frequently applied, they become the norm for how the two teams work, and this is the best way to embed the code. The code can be reviewed, amended, added to at team meetings, so it becomes a living process. As an aside, but very important point, the context for the code, as I have introduced it, is at the start of a new engagement, in the integration stage of the lifecycle. It can, however, be introduced at any time. Supplier relationships can get broken, for example, half way through a three-year contract. Introducing the idea of the working code is an effective way of pressing the reset button to reboot the relationship.

## Before You Sit Down with the Supplier to Discuss the Code

While you should consider what you might want included in the code, it is important to remember that the code must represent a jointly agreed set of statements to make it meaningful. Working with a new supplier, on a new engagement, is an opportunity for you to look at your team—to study the current behaviors, what works well, what could work better. You can then consider what you want to change and put forward ideas for the new joint code.

A new supplier also provides the opportunity for you to take on board their behaviors that you feel are positive. An agreed upon way of working does not mean that you want them to be 100 percent like you. In fact, there can be an opportunity in recognizing some differences as adding to the relationship. I recall a case from some time ago, when I was working with a client in the media sector. They were fun to work with, the pace was always fast, with lots of energy. Their decision making was extremely reactive, with little thought, which often meant that issues had to be readdressed a number of times. They selected a supplier for a major IT infrastructure development project for a key reason as well as their technical competence—the supplier had a very process-based culture, so they felt that this would bring some discipline to their somewhat chaotic way of working. Within six months of the contract start and after a number of disputes about the supplier being inflexible, not reacting to last minute change notice demands, frustrations about their complex processes, the customer managed to convert the supplier team to be like them—to be reactive, spinning priorities, and, consequently, missing deadlines, leaving end users feeling unhappy and dissatisfied with the service; in fact, just where they were before they decided to outsource the work. Hopefully, the learning point is clear: Suppliers can bring value to the relationship by having a different culture and way of working to your own. The following checklist will help focus your thinking before you sit down with the supplier:

- What do you see as your team attributes in terms of communication/behavior? *If these attributes work well internally, then can they be transferred into the code?*
- What do you see as your team deficits in terms of communication styles? *If there are deficits in terms of internal communications, could they impact communications with suppliers?*
- Where do you feel the supplier needs to have common characteristics as you? *Where do you think it is important that you have similar intrinsic characteristics in terms of behavior?*
- Where do you feel it would be helpful for the supplier to be different from you? *You may want to introduce change so it can be beneficial for the supplier to be different from you in some areas.*
- From what you know of the supplier, where do you feel the common ground is—in behavioral terms? *You are some way into the lifecycle, so there should already be a view on this.*
- From what you know of the supplier, where do you believe there are differences that would not be positive? *You should already have a view.*

## How to Establish the Working Code

Let me paint a picture. You are responsible for the operational management of a new supplier initiative. The service delivery is scheduled for three months after a handover, transition period. The sourcing/procurement work is now finalized, and the initial operational kickoff meeting is scheduled for two weeks. The supplier delivery team members have not been very involved in the preprocurement stages of the lifecycle. While they would have been briefed by their presales colleagues, the meeting is designed to introduce them to you and your team, confirm key elements of the contract, required deliverables, timelines, review meeting frequency, reporting requirements, and so on.

In addition, plan to allocate one hour of the agenda to discuss and agree on a working code. As this is something you should assume that they will not be familiar with, send a note out beforehand, explaining what you want to achieve and why you think it is relevant and important.

In broad terms, the objective is to have a structured discussion to arrive at an agreed upon code of behavior toward each other, which we would aim to summarize in a 10-point *charter*. The focus must be on *how* we *behave* toward each other—not policy or process.

The agenda could run on the basis of these five questions:

*What are our expectations of you?*

▼

*What are your expectations of us?*

▼

*Where do we agree—what can we bank?*

▼

*What do we need to discuss and agree on?*

▼

*Can we describe our code in a 10-point charter?*

### What Do We Mean by Code? Why Is It Important?

For clarity, this can be summarized as follows:

- A set of statements of behavior
- Need not be complex—in fact, the simpler the better
- Mutually agreed upon—something we both can refer back to
- Once agreed upon, the code will make communications throughout the engagement much easier

## Establishing the Working Code: Examples of Behavior Statements

They are examples only, built up over a period. As previously suggested a code should consist of around 10 statements. Think of this list as a menu to choose from. You can delete, add to, amend to cater for your specific relationship and situation.

1. Do not assume—check your understanding by asking questions.
2. Listen to what the other party has to say.
3. Consider the other party's perspective when making decisions.
4. Acknowledge that the other party could be right.
5. Be factual and rational when resolving conflicts—respond not react.
6. Be open and honest in our communication.
7. Resolve disputes by discussion—resort to formal escalation as a final option.
8. Be proactive in identifying and handling risk.
9. Own up if we get something wrong.
10. Negotiate in a balanced way—an agreement must work for both parties.
11. Recognize the other party's constraints.
12. Be clear when we cannot negotiate or move on a point—explain why.
13. Accept factual and balanced feedback from each other.
14. Welcome ideas from the other party—encourage innovation in thinking.
15. Appreciate that our respective company cultures may be different.
16. Give sufficient notice of complex/difficult conversations—no surprises.
17. Jointly address problems with a solution focus—avoid the blame game.

18. Use the contract as a positive frame and reference for both parties.
19. Approach changing requirements and priorities (of the customer) positively.
20. Positively challenge, and accept positive challenges.

Some key reminder points:

- The purpose of the list is to provide you with some ideas—adapt, add to for your specific suppliers.
- One joint, mutually agreed upon list is important.
- It must be developed by discussion and involvement.
- Establish the code at the project/operational team level.
- It is helpful if there is a common code for all levels of the relationship.
- Keep it simple—start with a 10-point code.
- You can develop and change it over time.

Finally, a reminder that the code is about behavior—not process or contract. I have observed when facilitating discussions on generating ideas for the code that there is a tendency for people to fall back to process or governance areas—agree on review meeting agenda, ensure we comply with the change control process, draw up meeting schedule for key user representatives, agree on who draws up and circulates minutes of meetings, and so on. These are important but are *what* items—process, contract type issues. The code is about the *how*—if it not describing a behavior, it cannot make the code list.

### Thought Provokers

1. In your organization, what would be the challenges to establishing the working code concept with key suppliers?
2. To what extent do you feel suppliers might react with suspicion to the working code idea?
3. Why do you think that could be?
4. What actions could you take to introduce the idea?

## *Takeaways*

From a personal learning perspective, what are your three key takeaways from this chapter?

| 1 | |
|---|---|
| 2 | |
| 3 | |

# CHAPTER 9

# Cross-Cultural Working

*In this chapter: defining culture, some observations about cultural differences, implications of working with suppliers from a different culture to your own, ideas and tips for managing the challenges, including how to communicate remotely*

## Defining Culture

To set the scene, and to manage expectations, culture is a vast and complex topic. This chapter is intended to provide some very brief insights into its core principles and then focus on how the understanding of culture and appreciating the implications of working with suppliers from different parts of the planet than your own will help you manage those relationships most effectively. You will recall in the last chapter, establishing the working code, I touched on culture and provided the following definitions of corporate culture:

- *The way we do things around here*
- *The behavioral norms, what is accepted*
- *The way an organization communicates internally and to the outside world*
- *Behavior that is influenced by the values of the organization*

In this chapter we will discuss national cultures because these will influence the corporate cultures of the offshore suppliers that you are working with. To build on these four definitions, I would like to add in the following—*a system that enables individuals and groups to deal with each other and the outside world.*

An obvious implication of working with an offshore supplier is that they will be from a culture that has different values, traditions, beliefs, and behaviors to your own. It has been established in previous chapters that a good, positive working relationship is key to the success of an engagement. Understanding the respective cultures is a prerequisite for building the relationship.

In discussing different cultures it is important to remember that *no culture is intrinsically better than another. They are just different.*

It is important to highlight the risk of national stereotyping. As with all human and behavioral topics it is better to think in terms of tendencies rather than absolutes. There a few specifics on the dangers of stereotyping. First, is the risk of assuming that there is a national culture; I think that a country analysis is valid, but remembering that in countries there are differences. A Berliner would probably see themselves as being different from a Bavarian; in the United Kingdom a person from Liverpool would see themselves as being different from a Londoner; a resident of San Francisco would not see an absolute cultural fit with someone from Wyoming. Second, does the culture of a global corporate override national cultures? For example, does a Microsoft or Apple office feel similar be it in the United States, Eastern Europe, Japan, or South Africa? It is an interesting question. On the face of it the offices look and feel similar regardless of where they are and without doubt globalization appears to have made the different cultures *less different.* Under the surface, however, when you start talking with the people—and I do not mean language here—those differences are there.

Finally, coming back to the national level, a story to reinforce the risk of stereotyping: A German colleague of mine is one of the most random, unstructured people I have ever met; I have an Italian colleague who is planned, organized, and an impeccable time manager. So, in summary, we can use the *science* of cultural behaviors as a guide, and this is very helpful; however, use as a guide only, as judgment is required.

## Some Observations on Different Cultures and Behavior

I will start with some everyday, nonbusiness examples.

In Dusseldorf I am standing at a pedestrian crossing, with the light on red, but no car in sight in either direction. I start to cross with the light on red; I hear sounds of disapproval from other waiting pedestrians, so I comply, step back onto the pavement, and wait for the light to turn green. A few hundred miles south, in Rome, crossing the road is a matter of chance. The laws are pretty much the same as in Germany. In Italy, however, both drivers and pedestrians will judge the specific situation and make the decision to stop or not at a pedestrian crossing.

Why do Scandinavian countries feel different to other countries in Northern Europe? I appreciate here that I am categorizing all the countries in that region into one entity, which I am sure they would take exception to. The difference, however, is not about the weather (generally colder) and the cost of living (generally higher than other parts of Europe). Scandinavian countries just feel culturally different—the senses tell you that it is different to be in Denmark rather than Holland or Sweden rather than Germany.

Moving on to look at some examples in the business context:

- I was in Switzerland, talking with a German lady. We were talking generally about the different cultures within Europe, and specifically, discussing how analytical German and Swiss people are. She was married to a Frenchman. I made the comment that the French are quite analytical; she agreed but qualified it by saying "Yes, but in a different kind of way." As someone who has worked with many German colleagues, and lived part time in France for a number of years, I know exactly what she meant.

- I had accompanied a manager from the U.S. headquarters of a multinational to a meeting in Paris; the audience was made up of managers from the French operating company and other European divisions. His objective was to gain commitment to a rollout of a marketing program throughout Europe. The meeting was cordial enough, but I sensed that although the French sounded positive, they had reservations. On the way back to the airport the American was enthusiastic and was pleased that the French had been so positive. His view was that they had signed up. My view was that they had not directly said *no*, but had certainly not said *yes*.

- I have mentioned Scandinavia already in this chapter. I recall on a seminar I facilitated some time ago that there were some Southern

Europeans, some Swedish people, and a couple of managers from Finland. The two Finns had been very quiet throughout, to the point it was bothering me. Without any prompting during a coffee break, one of the Swedes said to me, "Do not be worried about the Finns being quiet; they are Finnish, they are behaving as normal, they are quite happy." Incidentally, before I get e-mails from people in Scandinavia, I appreciate that Finland is not seen as part of Scandinavia but is part of the broader Nordic region.

- On a number of occasions, I have heard managers from U.S. or European companies speak of their frustration with suppliers based in India. There was a theme: They had asked the supplier to complete some actions with some urgency. Their understanding was that the supplier had agreed to the request, only to be disappointed when the deadlines they thought the supplier had agreed to were not met. In most cases the issue was not with the competence of the supplier, but with the misunderstanding about what had been agreed to.

What do these stories tell us? Simply that understanding people from other cultures in terms of their values, thinking, and behavior is not straightforward. In the context of managing offshore suppliers there are risks to performance and the relationship if we cannot develop an effective way of working, which involves putting in place measures to address the cross-cultural complexities.

## Implications of Cross-Cultural Working

We have defined culture, what is meant by cross-cultural working, and looked at some typical examples of the possible challenges. So, what are the implications for managers who are managing suppliers based offshore and from a different culture from their own?

- The importance of a positive relationship, and the positive impacts this can have on supplier performance, has already been stated.
- To reinforce another previous point, a positive relationship cannot be developed without an understanding of the underlying values

and beliefs of the supplier organization.[1] If the supplier is based in a different part of the world to your own, in a country you are not familiar with, it means that you will be unable to make any assumptions—you will need to find out.

• The supplier's beliefs and values will influence how they communicate among themselves and with you. Considering the different geography, and the consequent beliefs and values, it is probable that their communication style will be different from your own.

• Offshore relationships mean that you are working at a great distance from the supplier team. While it is true that many large suppliers who are operating globally will have their account management locally based, this is not always so, and communication with the delivery team, which will be based remotely, is a key part of the relationship.

Building relationships with and communicating in an effective manner with suppliers can be a challenge. Add in the aforementioned factors and the challenges are magnified. To help you address these tasks the rest of this chapter covers the following:

• A model to provide an overall frame for analyzing different national cultures

• A guide for understanding different communication styles driven by culture

• Managing remote communications

• Agreeing on a cross-culture version of the working code

## Hofstede Cultural Dimensions: A Frame for Understanding Different Cultures

There are a number of studies on different cultures and their implications for building relationships and communication. As businesses have

---

[1]Building the relationship also involves gaining an understanding of their business drivers and motives and their strategy and objectives. These are not strictly cultural issues—in Chapter 6, I have already introduced the customer segmentation model, and in subsequent chapters these areas will be further developed.

become more global, this topic has become more relevant—and no more so than for managers in an organization whose roles include the management of suppliers from another part of the world.

The Dutch psychologist Geert Hofstede is a recognized leader in the field of understanding different cultures.

Hofstede published his cultural dimensions model at the end of the 1970s, on the basis of a decade of research. Since then, it has become an internationally recognized standard for understanding cultural differences. The research began when Hofstede was working for IBM. He studied employees from across 50 countries in the IBM world; the analysis, over a number of years, involved 117,000 staff. As this initial research focused solely on IBM employees, he could attribute those patterns to national differences and minimize the impact of company culture. Over the years more extensive research was conducted in a number of countries, involving a diverse range of employees in corporations, as well as students and civil servants. The original model consisted of four cultural dimensions; on the basis of the additional research and refinement of thinking, there are now six dimensions to the model.

The following are Hofstede's six cultural dimensions, with my brief explanations.

### Power Distance Index

This dimension is about the degree to which the inequality of the level of power and influence of groups and individuals in a society is the accepted norm by those with less power. For example, in cultures where there is a high acceptance of this difference you are likely to experience levels of hierarchy in family, general social and business structures. In companies there is likely to be a very vertical structure where individuals at their respective levels understand and accept the parameters of their authority and find it natural to refer to superiors for decisions outside of their direct responsibility. In a small power distance acceptance culture, hierarchy and formal positional power, and with it, official status is less accepted. In companies this culture will tend to be reflected in relatively fewer tiers of management, resulting in horizontal structures. An Individual's authority is not linked to position to the same degree. Exercising power on the basis of position is more likely to be challenged.

### Individualism versus Collectivism

This can be summarized as a *me* versus *us* orientation, be it at a broad social or company level. The *me* culture emphasizes the need for individuals to strive to achieve their own objectives, because the individual, their freedom of action, and their focus on themselves are seen as key elements of success. The collectivist culture has a far greater focus on the group, and the need for individuals in the team to work together, support each other, as success is viewed at a team not individual level. Implicit in the collectivist culture is the responsibility people must support other members of their group, be it their family, village, organization or colleague peers; in the workplace this translates into being a positive team member.

### Masculinity versus Femininity

Cultures with a high score in the masculine range of this dimension tend to demonstrate high levels of individual competitiveness, where the goal is to win at all costs and where the winning is exhibited by material reward. Success is highly prized in this culture. By contrast a culture with a high score on femininity reflects a softer culture that works on consensus and cooperation. Success at the material level is not as dominant as overall quality of life, a society that is caring and supportive of all members. In the workplace this can be observed in the way decisions are made, the degree to which consensus is important, and the degree to which there is a sense of a cooperation rather than competition among team members and between teams.

### Uncertainty Avoidance Index

This dimension measures the degree to which a society can accept and live with a lack of structure, with levels of uncertainty, and therefore, an environment that is difficult to predict. Cultures with a high score on this dimension work within highly structured organizations with high levels of process and a set of behaviors that support planning and analysis as a way of managing events. Cultures with a low score on this dimension are pragmatic, accept that much of the future cannot be forecast, and therefore, cannot be planned for. This acceptance means that such cultures are comfortable with ambiguity and a therefore confusing picture. In the workplace this can be observed, for example, in the way that risk is handled, the degree of process to mitigate risk, and the way in which decisions are made—say, only after in-depth analysis and all facts are gathered or a preparedness to accept not everything is known.

### Long-Term Orientation versus Short-Term Orientation

Societies with a long-term orientation are focused on the future and see the benefit of thinking of the long goal in terms of investment, education, persistence, perseverance, and demonstrating high levels of patience. These are accepted as ways of preparing for the future, with an appreciation that short-term sacrifice may be required. Short-term orientated cultures are more focused on the past and immediate future and are concerned to maintain familiar traditions; with this desire to maintain the status quo, changes in the society can meet with resistance. At an organizational level, the long-term orientation can be observed by the commitment to vision and strategy, the commitment to work toward long-term goals as opposed to a short-term orientation showing, for example, a focus on the next quarter's results and quick paybacks, potentially at the expense of the mid- and long-term plan.

### Indulgence versus Restraint

This dimension relates to the degree of discipline a society has. Cultures that score high on indulgence make room for people to express themselves and, follow their feelings and instincts to indulge and enjoy life. High-restraint societies have developed rules and regulations that impose restrictions, driving people to exercise control, and emphasize fulfilling duties. At an organizational level this can be observed by studying the stated values of the organization and how the people behave in the workplace—for example, making lighthearted comments about the organization, a sense of work hard/play hard or a more serious and task-focused culture.

These are my own very top-line descriptions and explanations of Hofstede's six dimensions.[2]

If you are involved in working with offshore suppliers, I strongly urge you to invest some time in studying Hofstede in more detail, to enable you to apply the principles his work contains.

I would like to reemphasize a point I have made before: We are discussing customs, beliefs, values, and behavior—this is not 100 percent science as in chemistry or physics. With behavior we should be thinking in terms of tendency—so if someone comes from a certain country it is likely that they will think and behave in a certain way. That does not mean, though, that every company in Singapore, for example, will demonstrate the beliefs and behaviors as per the dimensions in the Hofstede model. As with all behavioral models it provides a guide and some useful insights from which you can make your own decisions.

To help in the application of the awareness and knowledge that the Hofstede model provides, I have generated some examples of customer–supplier cultural differences and raised questions about the possible implications.

Situation 1: The customer organization is from a small *power distance* national culture. The organization has a flat organization structure, decision making is delegated, and there is a general feeling of empowerment among team members. The supplier organization is based in a country with a large *power distance culture*. The organization is hierarchical, there are clear lines of control, and most decisions must be referred to one or two levels for sign off. *Thought provoker:* What are the potential stumbling blocks for an effective working relationship?

Situation 2: The customer organization reflects the national culture of its parent company. It is a highly competitive environment where

---

[2]To gain more insight into the work of Geert Hofstede, the following sources will be helpful:

Geert Hofstede, Gert Jan Hofstede, Michael Minkov. Further reading—"Cultures and Organisations, Software of the Mind," Third revised edition, McGraw-Hill 2010, ISBN 0-07-166418-1.

http://www.geerthofstede.eu

https://geerthofstede.com/research-and-vsm/dimension-data-matrix/

individuals are expected to assert, to take calculated risks and make decisions, and would expect to be acknowledged and rewarded in doing so. The supplier organization reflects the national culture of its home country. The style of operation is based on working harmoniously, with discussion and consensus as the preferred decision-making process. The two organizations represent different positions on the *masculinity versus femininity dimension*. *Thought provoker:* What are the potential frustrations for the customer? What are the potential concerns for the supplier?

Situation 3: The customer organization scores *highly on the uncertainty avoidance index*. There are rigorous processes to ensure risks are minimized and decisions are made only when all the available facts have been analyzed. The supplier has a more pragmatic culture and scores *low on the uncertainty avoidance index*—there is an acceptance that we do not live in a perfect world and that some decisions need to be made without all the facts being available. There is an acceptance of ambiguity. *Thought provoker:* How is this cultural difference going to impact the trust the customer has in the supplier's approach to problem solving? What are the implications for trust?

The Hofstede cultural dimensions can help you understand the possible relationship implications when considering engaging with an offshore supplier; they can also provide some insights where you are already working with such a supplier and things are not working out too well. On Professor Geert Hofstede's website (www.geerthofstede.com) you can find more information and some instructive videos that explain the dimensions.

MindTools also have useful information on the application of the Hofstede dimensions (https://www.mindtools.com/pages/article/newLDR_66.htm).

## Culture and Communication Styles

In my experience, if you ask the question of people in a range of public sector bodies, large corporations, SMEs, educational establishments, and so on, "What do you feel are the factors that influence or impact the effectiveness of the organization?" invariably included in the top three answers will be "effective communication, or lack of it." This is not surprising—organizations are made up of people, and organizations depend on those people working effectively together to enable them to achieve goals. For individuals to work effectively in teams they need to be able to communicate effectively.

Achieving effective communication, a prerequisite for positive working relationships, is difficult in an organization. The challenge is greater in the context of a customer and a supplier organization, with their individual business interests, and even greater when the two organizations are from different national cultures.

An important point to make here is that in the discussion about communication there is an assumption that there is a common business language, so if the customer is based in Germany and the supplier in China, then the supplier delivery team members, or at least those with a customer facing role, have a good command of German. Of course, there would be an appreciation that the supplier team members, while competent in German, would not be communicating in their first language.

So, assuming competence of the required language, the challenge is understanding that different beliefs, values, history, and social norms that make up a culture result in differences in communication style. So, for example, an American and a French person who is fluent in English will communicate in English, verbally and in writing, in very different styles. This is about the cultural difference.

Style differences influenced by culture are explored in the concept of high-context and low-context cultures. This concept was introduced by Edward T. Hall in his 1976 book, *Beyond Culture*. Essentially, in a low-context culture the message, written or verbal, will be interpreted through the words, as the language and style are explicit. In a high-context culture the interpretation of the message is more complex, as in addition to the words the tone, gestures, implied meaning, background, and overall situation are all factors to consider. In other words, it is also important to consider what has not been said.

If we consider that any message has the following two elements, this can help our understanding of the two levels:

- **The content**—the substance of the message, that is, the facts, the ideas, the proposals
- **The context**—the history, the situation, the setting, the preamble, the background thinking

In general terms:

- The lower the context, the more direct the communication will be perceived as—characterized as being *clear, factual, explicit, concise, precise, views clearly stated, literal.*
- The greater the context, the less direct the communication will be perceived as—characterized as being *implicit, a subtlety of meaning, views, and feelings need decoding, therefore, requiring the listener to interpret.*

I have made the point before, but it is important, so I will restate: In describing behaviors we should think in terms of tendency rather than absolutes. For example, high-context communication tends to be prevalent in long-established societies or organizations; because relationships are well established, some of the messages in a communication are implied, as the recipient will know how to interpret what is being communicated without it actually being directly stated. Low-context communication tends to be more in evidence in societies and organizations where there is less background, less history, less tradition. Considering the lack of experience of being together, the communication has to be clear and explicit so that the interpretation is not left to chance.

This is a simple principle but is profoundly important in terms of how customers and suppliers from different cultures communicate. The following pages give some insights into the different cultures and their communication styles.

The characteristics of the two communication styles can be summarized in the following way.

### High Context: Behavior Checklist

- Implicit
- Indirect
- Polite
- Feelings and views require interpretation
- Subjective
- Relationships considered important
- Intuitive
- Assumes the recipient will be able to interpret

### Low Context: Behavior Checklist

- Explicit
- Clear and direct
- Views and feelings openly communicated
- Communication rules are commonly understood
- Assumption of what is said is what is meant—literal
- Transactional
- Objective
- Focused on the topic/task
- Logic based
- Detailed

There are clear implications if there is no awareness that these differences exist and steps are not taken to mitigate the risks involved. I will address this later in this chapter.

## Where in the World? Which Communication Style?

Logically this is the next question to answer. With my usual caveat of oversimplification being dangerous, there are some general indicators to allow us to make style–geographic links. In general terms:

- The United States, Northern Europe, including Scandinavia, are low-context cultures.
- Southern Europe has slightly more context but in global terms is still relatively low context.
- India, Africa, and Latin America are in the middle of the spectrum on the context scale.
- The Middle East is a moderately high-context culture.
- Asia represents a high-context culture.

Within each of these categorizations there are, in reality, many subdivisions. Asia consists of many nations and millions of people. Japan and China are in the same category, but there will be differences in detail. As with all behavioral topics, it is best to think of tendencies rather than absolutes on a scientific scale. For example, to an American, a Middle East communication culture would appear as high context; to a Japanese, it would seem, in relative terms, less higher than their own style. To illustrate the potential nuances, here is a breakdown of Europe, my home turf, so the analysis is particularly interesting.

## The European High-/Low-Context Map

High context—Spain, Greece, France, Ukraine, Slovakia, the Czech Republic, Estonia, Italy, Portugal, Turkey, Romania, Hungary, Russia

Low context—Austria, Switzerland, the Netherlands, Finland, Denmark, Germany, Ireland, United Kingdom, Norway, Sweden, Poland, Belgium

For clarity, on a global scale, all of Europe is placed in the low-context category, but even within different low context countries there are differences. To provide a personal experience of the differences even within the lower context countries of Europe, some time ago I was working in Germany with a team working on IT development. A few months earlier, due to organizational changes, the UK office had been closed and the staff relocated to Germany. So the team, numbering around 40, was roughly half German and half British. Over a coffee one morning one of the German team members said to me, without any rancor or bitterness, "You know the Brits can really be putting the knife in, but it feels OK." What did he mean? As a Brit myself I understood straightaway. Had a German colleague been, as he said, putting the knife in, he would have known because the conversation would be very direct, explicit, the message would be 100 percent clear. The British approach is not so direct, as they tend to circle around a topic, possibly apologize for raising a concern, maybe even stating it is not that important but felt it needs airing , and so on before finally getting to the point. Hence, the observation from that German team member—he had a lot of interpreting to do with a communication from a British colleague, which would not be the case with a German colleague. For the record, I totally appreciate that the British lack of directness can sometimes frustrate our European colleagues.

# How to Manage the Differences

**Low to high:** If you are from a low-context culture, what to consider if your supplier is from a high-context culture:

- Acknowledge the status of the individuals involved. A high-context communication is often experienced in an Asian culture, where there is a clear hierarchy in the organization. Be aware that decision making is probably less delegated.
- Linked to the first point, if someone is not able to make a decision (because of hierarchy), it may not be obvious that this is the reason—you may need to interpret, and check out your understanding.
- Be aware that *yes* does not always mean *yes*; it could just mean that it is not *no*. In Asian cultures *face* is important so admitting I am unable to do something, or do not have the authority to sign something off, is difficult. Also, an outright *no* would be seen as being impolite.
- Relationships tend to be more important in high-context cultures; taking time to establish a relationship is seen as an investment.
- Balance a possibly preferred approach for directness and decision making with diplomacy—this is linked to the previous point.
- Take time to clarify what the mutual understanding of what has been agreed upon is.

**High to Low:** If you are from a high-context culture, what to consider if your supplier is from a low-context culture:

- You can take things at face value—what is being said to you is what is meant to be said.
- Be as explicit as you can—hints may not be noticed.
- In communications, concentrate on the task.
- Ask direct questions to clarify your understanding, as they will not be seen as offensive.
- Do not necessarily equate authority and decision making with status in the hierarchy.

How can this awareness and knowledge help in managing suppliers from different cultures effectively? Assume you are working for a global investment bank based in mainland Europe. The culture in the bank is very business focused; to drive down costs the hierarchy has been stripped out in recent years, so the organization though large is flat. There is a strong project focus in your part of the business—IT support and infrastructure development. Timelines are clearly defined, there are rigorous processes, and it is expected that outcomes will be delivered on time. A year ago, the decision was made to outsource certain support services to a specialist offshore provider in Asia. Over the last two months the first service delivery package was transitioned over to the supplier, with an expectation that the handover would be seamless; all training was done beforehand, and you were comfortable that the delivery team members were well selected by the supplier and competent for their allotted roles. Conversations are harmonious, no request is challenged; everybody in the supplier team seems very committed. You, however, are experiencing problems. Deadlines are being missed, and you are receiving critical feedback from your customer stakeholders. Is this about competence or culture?

I paint this picture purely to demonstrate the relevance of the understanding of the different communication styles to real world issues. There is no single answer, but see the final part of this chapter for some suggestions—agreeing on a cross-cultural version of the working code.

## Managing Remote Communications

We have already discussed that effective communication is imperative for a positive customer–supplier relationship; also, we have agreed that establishing good, effective communication can be a challenge in any business situation. Add in the fact that we are now involving two organizations, with different cultures, and by the very nature of an offshore engagement you are not in the same time/same place as the supplier. Being able to communicate from a distance in an effective way that creates and maintains a positive working relationship is, therefore, a key skill requirement for supplier managers. The following checklist emphasizes the remote context but should be considered alongside all the other communication areas covered in other parts of the book.

*Guidelines for Remote Communications: 15-Point Checklist*

1. **Communication code:** In establishing the working relationship pay special attention to developing the communication code of practice. Summarize this into no more than 10 key points.

2. **Think more:** Think before you act is always important. With remote management this is key—you cannot walk over to a desk to say, "Sorry, I got that wrong" if there is a misunderstanding.

3. **Consider the best mode/method:** Accepting that face to face is not possible, consider the message and the significance of a communication. Resist just firing an e-mail—pick up the phone whenever possible for any communication that is more than *routine*.

4. **Use multiple media:** For any significant communication send an e-mail first to give context/background, use the phone to discuss and to make decisions. Maximize the use of tools such as WebEx or Zoom after first ensuring that the supplier team is familiar with video conference meetings.

5. **Avoid surprises:** Give people advance notice of the need to set up a meeting. Any significant messages need to be thought through, and not just using e-mail.

6. **Signpost your communications:** Signposting is about signaling the move from one topic to the next in a communication. This is important in face-to-face communications, more so in remote situations.

7. **Label your behavior:** Similar to signposting—you are letting the supplier know where you want the conversation to go, and how you want to approach it. For example, "I now want to *brief* you on some internal changes we are making and then get your views on how you will manage this." Again, important in all communications, more so in remote.

8. **Schedule formal reviews:** A scheduled review is an opportunity to step back to review the broader relationship not just the immediate issues. Wherever possible these should involve visual as well as verbal communications—signals a difference from the day-to-day communications.

9. **Keep them updated:** The scheduled review is the vehicle for this. A remote supplier can quickly feel that they are out of touch, so take time to provide them with updates, not just on their specific

functions, but on a general *what is happening in the business* basis. This creates a sense of being involved, being part of the team.

10. **Respect/appreciate time differences:** Schedule discussions acknowledging time differences. For example, for reviews alternate times so that both parties share any inconvenience.

11. **Balanced feedback:** Of course this is important in any business relationship, but where the supplier is remote it is even more so. You will be less able to *pick up* signals of discontent/motivation issues due to inappropriate/unbalanced feedback.

12. **Establish some ground rules for your conference calls:** In much the same way as agreeing on meeting formats, agree on how the agenda should work for a conference call, the dos and the don'ts— not as a formal policy, more about how we work together.

13. **Make the most of face-to-face meetings:** These opportunities may be rare so make the most of them. Ensure you balance reviewing the past with looking at the future. Take the opportunity for team relationship building. Make these meetings special, by, for example, having specific agenda items, guest speakers.

14. **Consider their culture/working practices:** This again is always important, but if you are working in the same place as a supplier you will be always reminded of it, so you will be conscious of it. With remoteness this can be forgotten.

15. **Generally slow down:** Face-to-face communication is the easiest—in terms of checking out understanding, how your message was received. Remote makes it more difficult, so accept that communication make take longer, and it may need to be checked/reinforced.

The goal should be to create the same level of communication effectiveness with a remotely based supplier as if their offices were next to yours. It is a stretch goal but with awareness, skill, and clever use of technology it is possible to get very close.

## Agreeing on a Cross-Cultural Version of the Working Code

In Chapter 8 I established the importance of agreeing on our mutual expectations of behavior toward each other; the rationale and logic being that the optimum supplier relationships are based on a balance of managing the contract and establishing a positive working relationship. In this chapter we have discussed the additional challenges of building a positive supplier relationship where different cultures are involved.

The additional challenges and complexity of a cross-cultural engagement make the need to agree on a working code especially important for the simple reason that the working code focuses on desired behavior and the cross-cultural dimension increases the risk of *behaviour mismatch*.

The guidelines and outcomes regarding the code are the same as those covered in the last chapter, with the following additional points:

- It may take more time to introduce the concept of the code with some offshore suppliers depending where they are based and what national culture they belong to.
- For suppliers from a culture where there is a high *power distance index* score you may need to coach them and encourage them to feel empowered to contribute to a code on a joint/equal basis.
- Linked to the previous point, there is a risk that even though the supplier says they understand the concept, if the code is based on your input only, they may not be committed to it.
- Be prepared to share your thinking on the possible cultural differences and their possible implications.
- Once the code is agreed upon be aware that it will take additional effort to ensure that it is implemented and reinforced over time.

## Cultural Awareness: Quick Reminder/Checklist

- Be aware of the cultural/communication differences when working with suppliers from other parts of the globe.
- Remember no one culture is better than another—they are just different.
- Consider that what may seem strange to you is natural for someone from a different background.
- Be aware of the dangers of stereotyping—the country where the supplier is based is only one factor in influencing their behavior.

- The market, the corporate culture, other external factors will also influence behavior.
- Developing a behavioral code with an offshore supplier may take more time than with an onshore supplier—but the need is greater.
- Ask questions—take time to find out more about the supplier's behavioral style and norms.
- Be prepared to adapt your own communication style—this is not a sign of weakness but a focus on developing a positive relationship for both sides.

### Thought Provokers

1. In your organization, to what extent is culture considered when an offshore supplier is being engaged?
2. To what extent do you feel Hofstede's cultural dimensions could have helped with previous offshore supplier engagements that you have been involved in?
3. In your experience, where there have been issues with offshore suppliers, would you attribute them to lack of competence or cultural misunderstandings as the prime cause?

### Takeaways

From a personal learning perspective, what are your three key takeaways from this chapter?

| 1 | |
|---|---|
| 2 | |
| 3 | |

## Suggested further reading

Gupta, S. 2008. *Understanding Indian Culture and Bridging the Communication Gap*. London, UK: Subodh Gupta. ISBN 978-09556882-5-6

Hofstede, G, G.J. Hofstede, and M. Minkov. 2010. *Cultures and Organisations—Software of the Mind.* New York City, NY: McGraw-Hill Education. ISBN 978-0-07166418-9

Meyer, E. The Culture Map. New York City, NY: PublicAffairs. ISBN 978-1-61039 276-1

Mole, J. 2003. *Mind Your Manners.* Hachette, UK: Nicholas Brealey Publishing. ISBN 1-85788-314-4

# CHAPTER 10

# Supplier Communication and Influencing

*In this chapter: importance of communication and influencing, similarities and differences between managing in-house teams and suppliers, different relationship phases, factors that influence your communication style, communication and influencing styles model, case studies, communication style selection checklist*

## Communication and Influencing: Why Are They Important?

- In the day-to-day management of the supplier and their performance you will have numerous conversations on a variety of topics and issues—in this chapter I will cover a range of these.
- How you approach these conversations in *behavioral terms* will have a profound influence on the outcome. This is a key point. In any communication the objective is to reach a positive outcome for both parties in the most time-effective manner, and the style and behavior will influence how this is achieved.
- How you communicate will influence the relationship; we have already established that relationship and performance are linked.
- There is no wrong/right, good/bad behavioral style. The skill is in being able to flex your style to address the specific issue/challenge most effectively.

# Similarities and Differences between Managing Suppliers and In-house Teams

Most of the people I meet on supplier management training workshops have experience in managing internal project or functional teams; they have little or no experience of managing suppliers, hence their presence at the workshop. To try and remove the mystique of their new world of supplier management I often start by asking them what they believe are the similarities and differences between managing an in-house team and a supplier. Typically, the ideas and responses I get are as follows:

### Same/Similar

- Working with people
- Building relationships
- Working to clearly defined objectives
- The need to achieve those objectives
- Regular review of performance
- Agreeing on action plans and accountabilities
- Solving problems
- Regular and ongoing communication
- Managing performance, and specifically nonperformance
- Providing feedback
- Handling changing priorities

### Different

- Suppliers are in a different location
- Different company—maybe different commercial interests
- Not involved in ongoing staff training and development
- Not so involved in the detail

What do the lists tell us? First, the same/similar list is bigger than the different list. This is reassuring for the people in the workshop as it is clear that much of what they already do, their knowledge and experience can be transferred to their new role of managing suppliers. What it says is that management is management—it is about managing processes and people to enable you to deliver results against a set of objectives. The different list while smaller is very significant. We have already discussed remoteness and different location in the last chapter, specifically in the context of off-shore suppliers; however, in most cases all suppliers will be remote, albeit within the same country. The fact that there are two companies involved is interesting. If you are managing an in-house team it is reasonable to assume that the team shares the company's overall goals, strategy, and objectives—so there is a shared and commonality of purpose. When managing a supplier, however, while it is reasonable to assume that the supplier team you are working with is aligned to the service delivery or project objectives as described in the contract, it might be influenced by the broader supplier organization objectives. For example, how much pressure are the team members under to ensure that the budget allocated for the agreed service delivery is not overrun? If another customer demands more resource, could there be pressure to take resource from the team servicing you? Could their response to a change request be influenced by how much cost could be involved (for them), particularly if their ability to charge you for the requested change is limited? These are not necessarily problems, just potential complexities to be aware of.

The final two points in the different list are particularly important. Specifically, on training and development, while you, as the customer, might be involved in initial induction/orientation training to the specific contract/project, introduction to your company, and so on, ongoing staff development is the responsibility of the supplier. The people are a resource for you; the supplier must ensure that the resource is competent. The final point on the different list is *not so involved in the detail*. What does this really mean? It means that you, as the supplier manager, are not involved in managing activities as this is the role of the supplier. Your job is to manage outcomes. This final point is so key, I will reemphasize it.

*\* Your role as a supplier manager is to manage outcomes, not activities. \**

In a sense, outsourcing to a supplier is no more than a delegation. There will be times when you will have to take action, possibly go into micromanagement mode—I will be discussing such situations later in this chapter—but as a default, managing outcomes not activities is the rule.

# What Are the Topics of the Conversations We Have with Suppliers?

There is no precise answer to the question, as this will depend on the nature of the supplier, what service they are providing, and your specific role in the supplier management function. Generically, however, it is reasonable to assume that communication will be ongoing, a combination of scheduled and planned meetings and spontaneous, reactive dialogue, covering a range of topics.

In considering the topics, if we go back to the start of this chapter, to where we covered the difference between managing in-house and supplier teams, typically what sort of communications would take place with an in-house team? The answers are numerous—one-to-one progress checks, team briefing on the day's priorities, reacting to crises, planned review meetings, dealing with requests from customers or other departments, responding to changing priorities, handling specific project activities, providing and receiving feedback, and so on. Some of these communications will be planned, some not; some will be quick and simple to fix, some less so. All will have varying levels of importance and urgency labels. If we transfer that question to what sort of conversations do we need to have with the supplier, the answer will be largely the same. In summary, a range of topics, varying levels of formality, ranging levels of importance and impact, some planned in advance, some responding to immediate situations.

# Factors That Influence the Behavioral Style and Approach to Be Taken

Considering the range of topics identified, no single communication style will be appropriate and most effective in all situations. There are a range of factors, as follows, that will influence, and in some cases, determine the style of behavior:

- The relationship that has been developed between the two teams
- Experience (you believe) the supplier has on the specific point in question

- How long the question/issue has been outstanding
- The importance/significance of the topic or issue
- Your overall confidence in the supplier
- The amount of pressure you are under to resolve an issue/get an answer
- Time pressures and other constraints

Some of these are situational, while some relate directly to that supplier and the relationship that exists.

The maturity of the relationship will be a key factor—the following 3xS model is a way of visualizing this:

- **Phase 1:** Start—the early stages
- **Phase 2:** Stable state—after settling in period, for the majority of the contract term
- **Phase 3:** Severance/(Re)Select—the final period of the contract where the exit or contract renewal takes place

These relationship phases are all set in the context of the *deliver* stage of the lifecycle. The Start comes immediately after the *integration* stage of the lifecycle, and in fact, may often be seen as coming into play during the *integration* phase itself. Phases 2 and 3 are in the *deliver* stage of the lifecycle. In Phase 3, if a possible reengagement is the objective, we go back to the start point of the lifecycle itself.

These phases apply regardless of contract length—for example, in a three-year contract Phase 1 could be 4 months; Phase 2, 26 months; and Phase 3, 6 months. It is a frame to illustrate a logical, notional relationship path—it is not predicting, for example, that in the stable state there will never be uncertainties. At each stage there are possible positives/negatives, opportunities and risks.

The following table provides a list of the possible characteristics and behaviors to be found in each of the three phases. The potential positive and negative characteristics highlight the need for being objective in your assessment. Your conclusions will provide guidance to the most effective style and approach to take with the supplier, and at the same time, provide red flags if negatives are identified.

# Possible Behaviors of Supplier at Each Phase

### Start

- *Positive*—new, fresh ideas, innovation, keen, enthusiastic, relationship development performance progressing
- *Negative*—learning curve, do not understand customer organization, cultural differences, confidence in their ability is low

### Stable

- *Positive*—relationship established, mutual confidence, evolving performance, continuous improvement, understanding of the organization
- *Negative*—initial enthusiasm gone, early expectations are not met, disillusionment, complacency sets in, lack of innovation, supplier settles into maintenance mode

### Severance/Reselect

- *Positive*—supplier keen to renew, future discussion, open RFI/RFP process, refocus, supplier responds actively to challenge, opportunity to refresh KPIs
- *Negative*—supplier sees threat, looks for new customers, loss of focus, risks to service or project delivery, deteriorating relationship

The model (see Figure 10.1) illustrates a spectrum of styles available to supplier managers in their communications with suppliers. The model is based on the degree of push and pull behaviors applied. There is no single right or wrong approach. The skills in applying the model involve the following:

- Style flexibility—being able to move between styles dependent on a range of factors in a situation
- Judgment—deciding which approach to adopt in any given situation
- The model is intended to illustrate a spectrum of behaviors; as behavior is not black and white the scale describes different levels of push and pull, and highlights that there are shades of gray between the extremes.

The diagram below shows a spectrum of communication styles. It illustrates degrees of pull / push communication styles.

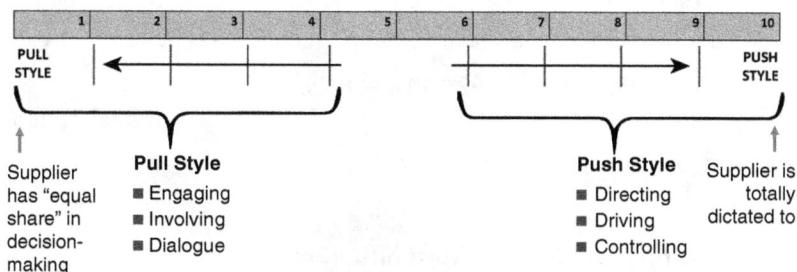

*Figure 10.1  Communication and influencing model illustrates the range of styles based on degrees of directing and engaging*

- The extreme push, *autocrat*, describes behavior where not just the *what* is described, but also the *how*.
- The main difference between 10 and the other levels in the push mode is the tone and that it is more likely to be used to direct the *what* only before moving to the pull style to discuss the *how*. The fact that the reason and rationale for the mandate is likely to be explained totally changes the overall sense of the message.
- The extreme pull, *democrat*, describes democracy in the purist sense of the word; in this context, there is joint decision making, with an equal share in the process. This may mean that if the supplier expresses serious concerns about the direction the customer wants to take, then the initiative would not move forward.
- The extremes of *autocrat* and *democrat*, while having validity in some situations, should not be majority styles.
- Most of the time you should be in the 2 to 9 range, and it is possible that in any one conversation or meeting a combination of push and pull styles will be applied.
- The skill is being able to judge which style is the most effective one to deploy in that conversation or part of the conversation and being able to have the behavioral flexibility to move between the styles seamlessly.

- In a sense you always start in the right hand side push style purely because you need to be clear about the reason for the conversation—stating the reason, agenda, and so on. Once this is done you decide if you stay in push, or move to pull straight away.
- Your style decision should be based on the situational factors highlighted at the start of the chapter.

### The Most Effective Style in Most Situations

There is no right or wrong, simply what is most effective in a situation. As a guide, being able to demonstrate balance will help you to select the best behavior and influencing style in working with suppliers. The following list shows the behaviors that will be viewed positively by suppliers. I have stated many times that relationship is important; the more suppliers perceive the customer behavior to be positive, the better the chance of a positive relationship. The list also shows that behaviors in both the directing and engaging modes are positive and will be perceived as so by suppliers.

Behaviors that will be viewed positively from the right hand side of the model—directing. This style is represented in the 6 to 9 range of the scale. The closer to 10, and 10 definitely, will be perceived as too direct/authoritarian, so not viewed positively.

- Confidence
- Directness
- Focus
- Decisiveness

To demonstrate the point: *How comfortable is a supplier likely to be if their main contact with the customer, the supplier manager, is not confident, is indirect/ambiguous, gets easily sidetracked from the priorities that need to be discussed, and is not prepared to make decisions?*

Behaviors that will be viewed positively from the left side of the model—engaging. This style is represented in the 2 to 5 range of the scale. The closer to 1, the greater the risk of the behavior *possibly* being seen as weak and lacking in conviction.

- Openness
- Engagement
- Involvement
- Listening

To demonstrate the point: *How comfortable is a supplier likely to feel if their main contact with the customer, the supplier manager, is not open with them or open to ideas, will not engage in dialogue, does not involve them in discussing options to resolve issues, and does not listen?*

### Guidelines and Suggestions in Applying the Model

- As a default, be directive on the *what* and engaging on the *how*.
- It is generally easier to work left to right on the model than right to left.
- Use the supplier's energy not yours.
- Use the extremes sparingly, but do not discount totally.
- Be guided by the maturity of the relationship, but do not be bound by it.
- There are exceptions to all rules and guides.

These are straightforward, practical guidelines; I have detailed and explained these ideas as follows.

### As a Default, be Directive on the What and Engaging on the How

This is a logical way of achieving a balance in conversations and meetings with suppliers. Simply put, be very clear with a supplier about what you want in terms of an outcome, a solution to a problem, progressing a project, and so on and then move to the involving/engaging style to discuss and agree on how the desired outcome is to be achieved. It demonstrates clarity, focus, and openness. There will be situations where the default will not be appropriate—for example, you may not be sure about the *what* so would ask for the supplier input; there may be other times when it would be appropriate and expedient to direct on the *what* and the *how*. The default is a good start point for most situations.

### *It Is Generally Easier to Work Left to Right on the Model than Right to Left*

At first sight this second suggestion seems to be totally contrary to the first point. Let me explain. This is about avoiding starting and continuing a conversation in the extreme right, 9 to 10, autocrat mode. Imagine a situation where a customer is mandating to a supplier that as from next week the reporting frequency and format must change, and that this will entail the retrieval and analysis of much more base data than before. So, the supplier will say, yes of course, or the supplier might respond by saying that even if they could provide the enhanced reporting with current resources (which they cannot) the access to the base data is not possible because the customer's processes and systems are based on nonintegrated legacy systems that do not talk to each other. After a moment's reflection the supplier manager concludes: Oh dear, the supplier is correct. How could the conversation be restarted? The supplier manager could say to the supplier, "I have been asked to provide enhanced reporting as from next week; while I am clear as to what the request is, I am not clear as to what is involved, what additional work it would involve you in. Can we discuss how we can approach this?" The customer could have saved a lot of time by taking this approach in the first place. If, as a result of the discussion, the supplier has not provided any useful input, and yet the end customer is demanding the extra reporting, the supplier manager may need to move to autocrat/mandate mode—but at least knowing the implications and hurdles.

### *Use the Supplier's Energy Not Yours*

If you are in the right side of the styles model, you are using your energy; if you are in the left hand side of model, you are asking questions, and therefore, using the supplier's energy. Steve Jobs, founder of Apple, was acknowledged as being a visionary during his sadly all too short life. One of his observations in the context of employees was, "It is dumb to employ bright people and then tell them what to do; you take on bright people and then get them to tell you what to do." Replace the word employee with supplier and I think the same logic holds. Assuming that the supplier selection process in your organization is robust, then suppliers are hired because they have experience, competence, and expertise in their area—they have bright people.

### Use the Extremes Sparingly, but Do Not Discount Totally

A supplier manager working at the autocrat directive level is unlikely to develop a positive relationship with suppliers. The supplier manager working in the extreme democrat mode risks being seen by the supplier as weak and non decisive. The guide, therefore, is do not use the extremes unless there is a considered reason for doing so. However, in specific situations, these extreme styles may be necessary, or even desirable. For example, if a supplier has repeatedly missed some deadlines and in spite of their re assurances there is no evidence of a turnaround, their nonperformance is now risking a critical project delivery, and you have had several meetings using a pull style, then you make the decision to go into the autocrat micromanagement mode. At a point it could be the only option. Take example two, a very different situation. You have engaged a niche software consultancy to help you develop some optional solutions to support a significant and radical route to market strategy. Your internal stakeholders favor option A as do you. The supplier recommends option B as they feel that while option A is attractive, the risks around implementing it, in the timescales and with the funds available, are too great. They are a credible supplier, they have demonstrated high levels of competence and experience during the engagement. Is this a situation where a decision should be made in the democrat style—shared decision making? It would be a brave decision to go against the considered recommendations of an acknowledged expert supplier.

### Be Guided by the Maturity of the Relationship, but Do Not Be Bound by It

Common sense suggests that the style approach you take with a new, untested supplier would be different from the approach with a supplier that has been working with the organization over several years and has always provided excellent and timely service. On balance, a more push/directive approach would be most appropriate for the new supplier, less directive more pull style with the established supplier. As a guide, this is a good assumption, with the caveat that with all suppliers the more you pull and engage, the more value you are likely to get, and you are using their energy not yours. Some time ago I was leading a discussion in a workshop on this topic, and someone made a very interesting comment: Surely, they said, with a new supplier is it not a good idea to get their ideas when they are new? They can see our current systems and processes with a new set of eyes; we should capture their thinking before we have converted them to behave like us. This is very valid—so do not be bound by how you feel you should manage purely on the maturity of the relationship and the supplier's track record with you.

### There Are Exceptions to All Rules and Guides

I have included this last guide point to reinforce an important principle: While models and guides are useful and helpful, they cannot make a decision for you—your own judgment is necessary. In the world of supplier management there are a number of variables in a range of situations, so a guide for managers in terms of style and behavior can only be that—a guide. To refer back to the start of this chapter—there is no single right/wrong, or good/bad approach. A number of approaches could work to resolve a situation—the judgment call is about selecting the most effective one.

## Applying the Communicating and Influencing Styles Model

Finally, to help reinforce the learning and to provide the opportunity to think through how the styles model can be applied, there are six small case studies, each one describing a typical supplier manager situation or challenge that requires them to have a discussion with the supplier. You can decide how you want to approach this: initially look at each case, make your notes, and then go to my analysis where I have provided some thoughts as to how the discussion could be approached. You can then compare your conclusions with my suggestions—remembering there is no single right/wrong answer. If you are short of time, you can go straight to my suggestions; however, I believe you will learn more by thinking through the situations first.

Finally, there is a 20-point checklist that summarizes the key points from this chapter. In my suggested approaches to each of the six cases I have indicated the relevant numbers from the checklist that I believe relate most closely to the case.

1. You are six months into a three-year contract. There seems to be some conflicts among teams in the supplier organization. You sense that this could impact their operational performance. How are you going to approach this?

*Analysis:* There are very few hard facts in this situation. There is a sense of conflicts, and there is concern that this could impact operational performance in the future. This implies that there is no performance issue, as measured against KPIs, at the moment. As there is no definitive data there could be a decision to do nothing; however, as a general rule, if there is a feeling that a problem exists or will develop, then it probably will. As with all conversations, you need to start by clearly defining what you want to talk about, so in that sense you are on the push side of the styles model. Moving to the pull style very quickly by asking questions to check out whether your feelings are correct or not, labeling your concerns as feelings rather than facts (you have no data to base facts on) is important. *See checklist points 1, 10, 11, 12, 13, 15, 16.*

2. Over the last two months there has been a shortfall in performance against one of the KPIs. For the first 18 months of the contract there were no problems. You have flagged it at the last review meeting, and you were assured that action would be taken. The latest performance figures show no improvement. What do you do next?

*Analysis:* This is a clear underperformance issue that needs to be addressed. As the problem has been raised before and assurances given that the performance issue would be resolved, there could be a temptation to start the conversation on the push side of the styles model, and stay there to make it, in effect, a series of instructions of what actions the supplier needs to take and by when. While starting off in the push style, clearly stating the issue and emphasizing that the objective of the meeting is to agree on plans to restore performance is correct, moving to the pull style is most likely to lead to the most positive outcome. There are some key questions: For 18 months, performance was to standard, so what happened 2 months ago to change that? What actions have you taken since the issue was first raised to get the performance back to the previous level? Why have they not produced results so far? What additional actions are you planning? It could be that in spite of trying there are genuine constraints on the supplier, in which case other questions would also be required. What constraints do you have that are preventing you from performing? When do you think those constraints will be overcome? In the meantime what support can we provide to help you? Questions, questions, questions. It is important that the meeting concludes with an agreed upon performance improvement plan with more frequent reviews than previously, with a temporary move to more directive/micromanagement. *See checklist points 1, 8, 9, 10, 13, 14, 17, 20.*

3. Your supplier is performing to the agreed KPIs as defined in the SLA. From the outset, however, you felt that you are always in the driving seat, being proactive and suggesting new ways of working together. You are frustrated with this as you believe that the supplier should be adding value by being proactive. Is this an issue? If so, how do you approach it?

*Analysis:* Possibly, the first consideration is to decide whether this is a performance issue or not. If the basis of the engagement and of the contract is that the supplier has to simply meet the performance standards as defined in the SLA to be deemed to be performing, then there is no performance issue here. If, however, part of the selection criteria was that you were looking for a partner who would be innovative, share best practices, and add value by being proactive in promoting continuous improvement, and they claimed in their RFP response that they could add value in that way, then in the broader sense of the word, they are not performing. The answer to this question will determine the tone of the push style agenda setting, which involves stating that while performance is being met at the KPI level, the expectation of a more proactive supplier is not being met. So after the push style introduction, there is now the familiar suggested move to the pull style to involve and create a dialogue. Again, questions are key: What is your view of how the relationship is developing? To what extent do you believe you are providing the innovative thinking that was a central part of your proposal? What barriers do you feel there are to this happening? What mutual benefit do you see in the relationship becoming more proactive and strategic? An understanding of how the supplier views the customer in segmentation terms will provide some clues as to how willing the supplier is going to be to invest in the relationship. *See checklist points 1, 8, 9, 10, 16, 20.*

4. The supplier is always on the defensive. Any minor question you raise is treated as an attack. They always come to meetings armed with reports that show how they are meeting the milestones conforming to all key measures. This approach makes an open dialogue difficult. You were not involved in the selection process; you inherited the project and the relationship three months ago.

*Analysis:* There is no reference to performance, so we can assume the issue is about communication and relationship. In many ways, the tangible performance issues are easier to address as a meeting can be fact based. Considering the behavior of the supplier, how the conversation is started is crucial to avoid a seemingly paranoid supplier from becoming even more paranoid. The introduction, in push style with a soft tone, should state concerns about how the relationship is (not) working and a desire for an open conversation to enable both parties to press the relationship reset button. Considering the defensive supplier behavior, the initial statement about agenda for the meeting should emphasize that it is not about performance. This should provide some reassurance. The reasons for their behavior are potentially numerous—experience with predecessor in your role, their own culture, something you have done, they do not see they are being defensive but just providing data as they believe this is what you expect. After a discussion, agreeing on a new relationship moving forward should be the goal. A code of practice could be a useful tool to use here. The fact that you have been in the role only a short time gives you license to ask questions. *See checklist points 1, 8, 9, 10, 11, 12, 15, 16, 17, 18, 20.*

5. Your supplier has recently appointed a new team leader as their main point of contact with you. For the first year there were no changes, but this latest change is the second in six months. Also, you have noticed there has been more staff turnover in the developer team. This in itself is not a problem, but you feel that the new people coming on board are generally less experienced than their predecessors. You feel that you are investing a lot of time to get them up to speed, which you feel is the supplier's responsibility. You have a review meeting coming up and intend to raise the issue with the account manager.

*Analysis:* The initial task is to identify what the legitimate concerns are before calling a meeting with the supplier. For example, is the problem the rate of staff change? Is it the perception of the experience profile of the new people that has changed and is getting less? Is it a feeling that you are not being consulted on staff changes? I raise these questions as the supplier could claim that staffing is their worry, not yours, as long as they deliver to the performance standards as per contract. On a tangible level, it seems that the supplier expects the customer to invest time in getting their new staff up to speed on the contract—logically, this is a supplier responsibility. At a broader relationship level, is there a worry that other customers are being given a higher priority, and the more experienced staff are being allocated to other customers? If so, this concern needs to be explored, as at the moment it is an assumption. The agenda for this could be quite complex; hence, the need to think through how the positioning of the meeting is communicated, using a push style to start before moving quickly to the pull style of engaging/involving to discuss and get answers to the key questions, for example, the reasons for the increasing rate of turnover, how the customer can be involved with staff change decisions in advance, involvement in signing off new team members or at least agreeing on a qualification/experience profile, how concerns about future performance shortfalls could be addressed, balancing the responsibilities for induction of new staff. *See checklist points 1, 8, 9, 10, 11, 12, 13, 15, 16, 20.*

6. You have recently taken over the management of a reasonably significant service delivery that has been delivered by a supplier for the last 18 months. In your view, the KPIs are vague and ambiguous. The performance is patchy, and you sense that the supplier is using the lack of clarity as a way of avoiding the issues.

*Analysis:* The challenge here is how performance is objectively assessed and reported if the KPIs themselves are not clear and are open to interpretation. Before starting any discussion with the supplier about changing the KPIs, it would be wise to refer to the contract to determine what flexibility there is within the contract to change or modify KPIs. Next is the need to assess the actual issues these KPIs are causing—what is the degree of disconnect between the reporting provided by the supplier and the data received from, for example, customer satisfaction surveys? Once these questions are answered, the objectives and reason for a meeting can be communicated to the supplier. Moving from push to pull mode, the questions are, once again, all important: How does the supplier feel that the KPIs are working? What would they fine-tune? Which do they feel should be dropped? Which should be added in? Suppliers may be comfortable hiding behind vague KPIs, or they could be frustrated by them— if performance is always subjective, that can work against them. Moving to an action plan, it may be necessary to go back to push mode regarding KPIs that you feel are important but that the supplier is reluctant to take on board. Some may be must haves from your perspective. *See checklist points 1, 8, 9, 10, 11, 13, 17, 18, 19,* 20.

## Case Study Learning Points Checklist

1. The code of practice will be helpful in having these (particularly the tough) discussions.
2. Your communication style will be influenced by the relationship and its maturity, and by the specific topic/issue you are discussing.
3. There is no right/wrong, good/bad style—the skill is style flexibility and knowing the most effective approach in that situation.

4. Use the extremes—autocrat/10 and democracy/1 with caution.

5. As a default direct on the *what* and engage on the *how*.

6. Ensure the supplier knows what your default is.

7. There will be times when you go from the default—ensure you signal why to the supplier.

8. Use the supplier's energy not yours—they were engaged for their expertise.

9. You can use a number of points in the behavioral scale in one discussion.

10. Questions are key—the more questions you ask, the more you are positively challenging the supplier.

11. Differentiate between facts and views—do not represent your feelings as facts.

12. If you think there is a problem, probably there is. Address early, do not wait.

13. In a sense you always start a conversation by directing, by defining the topic of the conversation you want.

14. In terms of discussing the *how* it is easier to move from involving to directing (i.e., left to right on the scale).

15. Differentiate an actual performance issue from one that is not directly performance related (e.g., communication, relationship).

16. Take responsibility for your feelings—"I have a concern about the relationship issues" *not* "You are causing relationship problems."

17. Do not assume—for example, why a supplier is not performing—ask questions.

18. Take advantage of being new to a supplier relationship—in the first three months you have a clear license to question and challenge.

19. If something is fixed and is nonnegotiable, make it clear and explain why.

20. Make sure every discussion ends with an action—so in a sense you often go back to directing to clarify agreement and action.

### *Thought Provokers*

1. In your organization what do you believe is the predominant communication style applied to supplier relationships?

2. How will the concept of your job as a supplier manager to manage outcomes and not activities influence your approach to supplier communications in the future?

3. How will moving to an involving/engaging style with suppliers provide more value to the relationship for both parties?

## Takeaways

From a personal learning perspective, what are your three key takeaways from this chapter?

| | |
|---|---|
| 1 | |
| 2 | |
| 3 | |

# CHAPTER 11

# Performance Review and Development

*In this chapter: purpose of performance reviews, reviews at different levels, focus on the operational review, different types of operational review, review meetings best practice checklist, review meeting agenda, reviewing KPIs using KPQs, reviewing the qualitative aspects of supplier performance*

## The Purpose of Performance Reviews

In lifecycle terms performance reviews become a key aspect of the relationship at the integration stage, and throughout the deliver stage. Planned and structured reviews are essential for the effective management of supplier performance and also for relationship development. The frequency and depth of reviews will have been agreed upon as part of the contract during sourcing; effectively planned and managed reviews ensure that the necessary governance of the contract is implemented. The level of governance and the management time to be invested in it will be influenced by the category a supplier has been aligned to as per the supplier segmentation model.

In the next section of this chapter I will introduce the idea that reviews with strategically important suppliers need to be carried out at different levels. There will be some overlaps between the levels, which is normal and to be expected. This chapter focuses on the operational level review, as this is the level that is most involved with the ongoing supplier performance and the implications of underperformance for the organization. Ensuring there are links to the other level reviews is key, however.

The purpose of reviews, and specifically operational reviews, can be summarized as follows:

1. Review performance against the agreed upon measures as laid out in the SLA and KPIs, or for project-based engagements, project deliverables and milestones.

2. Agree on plans to address performance shortfalls. Performance review is a lot more balanced than identifying shortfalls—but addressing them to restore performance to target level is a key part of the role.

3. Solve specific operational issues at the operational level review wherever possible. In any contract there will be a prescribed escalation process if issues cannot be resolved at the level they are raised. The aim, however, should always be, wherever possible to resolve without escalation. Resorting to the contract as a default is not good for the relationship.

4. Identify issues that cannot be resolved operationally and must be escalated—this links to point 3. To repeat the rule: *Only escalate if you have to*. Working out solutions to issues at the operational team level builds a more positive relationship.

5. Enable both parties to provide feedback to each other. The review is the ideal platform for honest and balanced feedback with a focus on what are we both doing that helps performance and what we are both doing that inhibits performance. I cannot emphasize enough that it should be two way.

6. To proactively manage risk. While an important part of the performance review meeting is to analyze and discuss previous performance, looking forward is also important, particularly in how this will enable you and the supplier to identify potential risks for the next immediate period and make plans to mitigate or at least minimize.

7. Update supplier on changes in the business, and potential impacts. Involving the supplier on what is happening in your organization, specifically in how those changes relate to the services they are providing, will have two positive effects. First, they will have more context and background to understand where their service fits into your business; second, they will feel more involved, which is good for the relationship.

8. Look at opportunities to develop performance. This is about looking beyond performance as measured against the current KPIs, and looking more broadly at continuous improvement and the added value for both parties.

9. Discuss the future and develop the relationship. This is broad and future focused.

Items 8 and 9 are interesting—while absolutely legitimate that they form part of an operational level review, they can also form part of reviews at different levels.

## Reviews at Different Levels

The focus in this chapter is on the operational review process; however, connectivity across the different review forums is key. The following descriptions are generic, as each supplier/contract engagement will have its own governance/review process. The purpose is to highlight the need for communication—this was introduced in a previous chapter covering stakeholders and relationship owners. Generically, we have defined three levels—for each contract there could be a number of stakeholders/touch points at each of them.

### Strategic Level

The purpose is to ensure that the supplier is keyed into the organization's goals and strategic direction and understands their role in supporting these; also, to know what strategic direction the supplier has and how this may influence and impact the future relationship. The effectiveness of these senior level forums is determined by the level of openness displayed by each party. Senior management from the customer and supplier organizations take the lead in such meetings, although management from other levels should also be involved to provide details where required.

### Business Level

The purpose is to manage the commercial relationship between the customer and the supplier. To set a context for the word *commercial,* here the overall business relationship is about managing the performance of and the relationship with the supplier. The commercial relationship focuses on the contract, and the review is a periodic appraisal of how the contract is working for both parties, and discussing and agreeing on any changes (e.g., requirements, volumes) that require a formal amendment to the contract. The contract owners from the customer side typically include procurement/sourcing, possibly legal in case of significant contract updating, and management from the supplier management team, possibly the supplier relationship manager.

### Operational Level

The purpose is to manage the supplier's performance, ensuring that as a minimum the performance is to the level defined in the SLA and KPIs, and that they respond positively to changing requirements in the business. Operational level management involves hands-on dialogue, with frequent planned meetings and regular day-to-day communication, specifically where issues have been identified that cannot wait for resolution until the next scheduled meeting. The supplier delivery manager and specific project managers for project-based suppliers typically manage operational level review meetings. Representatives from customer and key user groups would also attend, but possibly on an exception basis rather than every meeting.

### Communications between the different level reviews

The review structure and role involvement will be different for each supplier and service delivery so the aforementioned explanation is intended as a general guide. Regardless of specific arrangements, however, for the multilevel review process to work effectively, open and regular communication is vital. There must be two-way communication between the levels: Key points and agreements from one level review needs to be communicated to the responsible managers for the other level reviews. Also, the manager responsible for each level review should be able to provide input to managers who manage the other level reviews. This two-way communication is vital if the customer is to have an agreed and consistent direction and approach in working with a supplier. This may sound obvious and common sense, but this does not always translate to common practice. I have known situations where the operational team members are desperately trying to resolve serious performance issues with a supplier, and at the same time, a strategic level meeting is taking place, from which the outputs are rosy and positive and there are commitments being made for future business.

For clarity it is wise to draw up a chart to ensure that all responsible are aware of meeting frequency and expected inputs and outputs. Meeting frequencies will again be dependent on a specific supplier, the service they provide, and mission criticality, but as a notional planning base the following can be considered:

- Operational: weekly/monthly (more on operational reviews later in this chapter)
- Business: quarterly
- Strategic: half yearly/annual

For each level the chart should define frequency, review owner, information to be provided to other review levels, and information expected from other review level meetings.

## The Operational Level Review

Considering the purpose of the operational review and its focus on managing the ongoing supplier performance, the frequency of, and involvement of the supplier management role in, these reviews will be more frequent compared with the other two levels. I have described the three different review levels; in fact, there are different types and levels within the label *operational review*.

**Red flag:** This review is not scheduled, but called as required—responding to a specific issue/problem that cannot wait for the next scheduled review. It is reactive, the aim being to maintain operational performance and/or mitigate negative impacts. Note: This highlights the importance of ongoing tracking of performance—spot issues early.

**The status check:** This review is scheduled; indicative frequency—weekly. It is of limited duration, with a focus on short-term closing down of actions, reprioritizing as required, tracking performance against the SLA/KPIs, handling any immediate performance issues, planning for the next seven days.

**Full operational review:** This review is scheduled; indicative frequency—monthly. It has a broader agenda, to enable stepping back from the immediate operational challenges and issues. It involves the review of the latest performance reports, addressing identified performance issues, proactively managing risk by discussing possible risks/problems envisaged over the next 30 days and devising mitigation plans. It looks toward the future—discussion on performance development, continuous improvement. Depending on the specific supplier and contract planning, an extended meeting on a quarterly basis can be useful to discuss a specific topic, invite a guest to present (e.g., a senior manager from the end users to give some insights as to how the service is viewed and valued, and what additional service would be particularly helpful).

Considering meeting frequency, and the remoteness of suppliers from the customer's office, 100 percent face-to-face meetings will not be possible or represent the best use of time. Face-to-face communication will always be best but use of the many virtual meeting platforms now available makes this less of an issue than historically.

Regardless of the media there are some well-established rules to follow.

### Best Practice Checklist

- Should be scheduled—not arranged only when there is a problem (apart from the red flag meetings)
- Should be structured to provide an opportunity to step back—important as most of the time at the operational level conversations focus on immediate problems and issues
- Should not be a forum to present full/detailed performance reports—these should be provided in advance by the supplier and studied; the meeting can then focus on specific points highlighted by the prereading
- Should be used to reinforce the contract and agreed upon performance measures—not in a confrontational and mandatory manner, but through a discussion about the measures and how they can be best achieved and exceeded
- Should provide an opportunity for genuine two-way feedback
- Should not present surprises for either party—issues and problems should not be stored up until the next meeting; manage them when they occur.
- Should balance reviewing the past and developing the future—reviewing the past is clearly important as it is the basis for

discussing supplier performance; however, learning lessons from the past is most effective if those lessons are applied to the future

- Should always be action focused
- Must provide feedback on key points and actions to other level relationship owners and other stakeholders

### Checklist: Suggested Agenda for the 30-Day Review

Core agenda points for all meetings:

- Review action points identified at last review—close down actions, update as appropriate, keep an action log if required.
- Review performance reports for the prior 30 days—specific points for discussion should be highlighted prior to the meeting. Check congruence/divergence with business perceptions feedback on performance.
- Discuss specific performance issues and document remedial action plan.
- Log agreed risks for next period, and identify potential risks. Put in place preventative action, contingency, and mitigation.

Other possible agenda points (not necessarily for all meetings):

- *Formally* step back and review the relationship: How is the working code operating? Do we need to develop it? I am using the word *formally* in the sense it is a planned agenda item not a very formal discussion—in fact, the least formal the better.
- Review of current KPIs: Are we measuring what we should be measuring? What do we need to change, fine-tune?
- Look beyond the KPIs: What are the opportunities to develop performance to deliver more value for both parties—the qualitative aspects of performance.

## Review of Current KPIs: The Value of KPQs

*Let me start with a question:* Have you ever had the feeling, *I see green, but feel red?*

For those of you who have experience in managing suppliers or in managing projects are possibly familiar with the traffic light system of performance reporting. It is a highly visual way of summarizing performance against an agreed upon performance standard—in the case of supplier management these measures are expressed as KPIs or project deliverables.

In broad terms the traffic light colors equate to the following performance levels:

GREEN: All is good; performance is at least to the required level against all measures.

AMBER: Largely, performance is to standard; there are some deviations, which are recognized and can be/are being addressed by the supplier team.

RED: There are issues because there are significant shortfalls of performance against one or more performance measures.

What is being expressed in the *seeing green but feeling red* statement is that while the supplier is presenting performance reports that show that they are performing to standard, as a minimum, across all measures, the supplier manager is receiving critical feedback from the users of the service expressing dissatisfaction. So, there is a serious disconnect—a supplier congratulating themselves, unhappy customers, and the supplier manager (as the conduit between the two) with a problem to solve.

This situation is not unusual: Supplier managers frequently face this challenge. The conversations can be difficult. Supplier manager: "I am receiving critical feedback from key user groups about poor service." Supplier: "If you look at our monthly performance reports, as measured against the agreed upon KPIs, we are performing to standard for every dimension."

A mechanism that can be used to have a constructive conversation with a supplier about current KPIs and performance is *KPQs or key performance questions.* The concept of KPQs was developed by Bernard Marr, and in fact, he originally used the *see green but feel red* phrase.[1]

---

[1] For further reading, visit his site: https://www.bernardmarr.com/default.asp

Before we look at KPQs and how to use them, it is important to understand why the supplier view can be disconnected from the customer view regarding performance. There are a number of possible reasons:

- We are working with a set of measures driven by the supplier—they proposed their standard SLA.
- The requirements at the start of the engagement were incorrectly defined.
- The business requirements have evolved, but the performance criteria have not been revisited.
- The KPIs are vague—so performance against target becomes subjective and open to interpretation.
- We are measuring things we do not need to measure.
- There are things we should be measuring but are not.
- The KPIs are too technically focused, therefore, missing the context of the business requirements.
- The easy option was taken—identify everything that is easy to measure and measure it regardless of relevance.

The conclusions: First, a KPI should not be agreed upon and fixed forever. Second, to ensure that the business/user requirements are being met, KPIs should be reviewed on a regular basis. This does not mean change for the sake of change, but there may be legitimate reasons to fine-tune, change, or even drop.

Returning to the question of supplier performance, using the KPQ approach will enable a logical analysis to assess if there is underperformance, can establish if there is enough objective definition of current measures, if there are subjective views about performance, and finally, can provide some guidance on resolving any issues.

### Quick Review: Check Out Understanding of KPIs

- Simply put, KPIs help us understand how suppliers are performing in relation to providing the services/deliverables as defined in the original requirements document.
- KPIs are often a subset of the SLA.

- They are driven from the performance targets section of the SLA.
- It is recognized that KPIs need to be stated in SMART terms to make them meaningful and measurable.

The KPIs will have been agreed upon during the sourcing phase. In my experience, in discussions with people in the operational supplier management role, they often feel that as the KPIs have been agreed upon in the sourcing phase and form a part of the legal contract, they have to live with them regardless of their relevance and effectiveness. Alongside this is a sense that the supplier can *hide* behind poorly constructed KPIs but as the contract is the contract, they cannot be challenged. Most contracts defined by procurement professionals, with inputs from the legal department, will include the facility to amend KPIs, within certain parameters, built in. Obviously, it is wise to check the contract before getting into conversation with the supplier on this.

## KPQs

Quote from Albert Einstein: "All I ever did was ask simple *questions*."

- KPIs are designed to provide us with answers.
- KPQs are designed to raise the most important *questions* that we need answers to.
- By going back to outcomes/objectives as originally defined, then asking the relevant KPQs, we can arrive at a set of focused KPIs.

Using the KPQ approach:

- Go back to the business/user requirements as described in the needs document.
- Ask one or two KPQs per requirement.
- The answer to the KPQ will help you focus on what needs to be measured, and may cause you to adjust/change current KPIs.

**Example:**

I have selected the following example as it is sufficiently generic for all readers to relate to it and its relevance, regardless of their specific field of expertise. It also highlights how KPQs can be used to address a perceived supplier performance issue and identify the reasons for the *see green, feel red* disconnect. Finally, it illustrates how using KPQs enables you to step back and look at the performance and performance measures in objective terms.

*The Situation—the background, the problem, the solution using KPQs*

The customer is an international consultancy and accountancy firm with operations in the United States, Europe, and Asia. The European division has outsourced the production of PowerPoint presentations for important client presentations to a specialist supplier in India. The actual customers are senior executives in the firm. The Asian supplier is very experienced in this niche sector; the turnaround times demanded by the customer during the contracting phase were challenging, and the supplier questioned them. The customer was insistent saying quick turnaround time is a key requirement, and after discussion, and with the supplier demanding a premium rate for the speed of service, a contract was agreed upon.

There is an agreed process for how the supplier is briefed, and in what format, by the requesting executive.

As quick turnaround was a key requirement, the KPI of providing finished presentation within 24 hours of receiving a concise briefing was agreed upon. The supplier is achieving this consistently, so reporting GREEN.

Feedback from senior executives in the firm is, however, critical—the presentations often need a high degree of amending and correction before presenting to the client. This involves the executives in checking and correcting, feeding back to the supplier before the final version can be produced. The user view of the service is that the 24-hour target is not being met, and they are using their valuable time in quality managing the supplier, so RED.

So, to follow the guide:

Key back to the requirement: *turnaround of presentations within 24 hours of a concise briefing being given*
Situation: *supplier reporting green, client feedback red*

*Possible KPQs*
- How important is quality compared with quick turnaround?
- Typically, how much notice does the executive get of a meeting with a client where a prepared presentation is required?
- In total, building in feedback, error correction, and so on, how long is it taking the supplier to get to the final version?
- How can we define a quality performance measure?
- Is 24 hours a realistic target if we are to achieve the quality we require within the budget we are prepared to spend?

Possible outcome—new or revised KPIs

The outcome was a revision of the current KPI and the creation of an additional measure, as follows:

- Turnaround time moved to 48 hours to allow for additional quality checks. It was established after talking with a representative sample of the end customers (the executives) that on average they received five to seven days' notice of a client presentation. Allowing for their workload and the need to get the briefing to the design company, it was agreed that the more notice they could give the designers the better—but 48 hours was reasonable. It was privately acknowledged that the previous 24-hour turnaround was unrealistic and that it came about because of overall poor time management by the executives—they were simply passing the problem down the line.
- A quality standard average 97 percent accuracy at first draft was agreed. While there is some subjectivity in this measure, the sense is that if only very few minor alterations were needed, there would be general agreement that the goal of right first time had been achieved. This performance can be assessed using periodic customer satisfaction surveys.
- There was an agreement to review the situation again three months after the change to the new measures.

This is a simplistic but real example that illustrates how stepping back, asking some KPQs can be more effective than simply confronting the supplier on performance.

### Example KPQs

I emphasize that these are examples only—in real terms a KPQ would be linked to a specific need.

- To what degree has the requirement changed since this KPI was introduced?
- How are the current KPIs aligned to the business objectives and scope of service?
- What area of performance does the business area want us to measure?
- What quantitative measure have you used elsewhere to capture performance in this area (question to supplier)?
- Are the current KPIs expressed in SMART terms, or is there some ambiguity?
- What do we, or the business, do with the data we collect from this KPI?
- If we were to dispense with this KPI, what would we want to replace it with?
- Do we have a quantitative measure here, but the business requires a qualitative assessment?
- Why are we asking the supplier to measure this?
- What is the cost and time involved in collecting and analyzing this data?

### In Summary, in Using KPQs and Verifying KPIs

- Go back to the requirements, business needs as defined in the requirements document.
- Define the *key* aspects of performance (do not try to measure everything).
- Using KPQs will help create focus.
- Gain supplier inputs—they have experience in the market and with other clients.
- Agree on how performance will be measured and how verification will take place.
- Review frequently—use KPQs to check/regain focus.

## The Qualitative Aspects of Performance

KPIs and other hard performance measures are important and an essential part of a commercial contract. I would add one caveat—and that is not to ignore what I call the qualitative aspects of supplier performance. Typically, KPIs cover the very tangible aspects of performance—for example, response times, first call fix rate, number of calls handled, on-time delivery, delivery within budget. These are, of course, important.

Moving away from these hard measures, if you ask a supplier do they provide a *value add* service, they will invariably say *yes*—particularly when they are still pitching for the business. What does this actually mean? In fact, do you want all suppliers to provide this value add? The answer to the second question is probably not, particularly if you see a very transactional relationship where noncritical services are being provided. For a supplier that you put in the strategic box, however, the answer would be different. Are you looking for more than delivery to the agreed KPIs for these mission critical suppliers?

For example:

- Demonstrating innovation
- Being proactive
- Introducing/sharing best practices from their market experience
- Introducing efficiencies, streamlining processes
- Investing time to understand future/changing business requirements
- Taking time to understand your strategy, to provide them with more context

If the answer is *yes*, then these four questions can help you decide if you are getting additional value from the relationship. To what degree does the supplier

**identify**—helps you understand and determine your needs;

**investigate**—supports you in evaluating those needs, generates possible solutions;

**implement**—works with you in deploying your joint resources most effectively;

**improve**—reviews to ensure that people, processes, and solutions are optimized?

Using the preceding examples and the identify/investigate/implement/ improve model, it is possible to have a positive conversation with a supplier about how you perceive their service and how you can work together on the value-added, qualitative aspects of their performance.

Finally, in this chapter, can qualitative aspects of supplier performance be measured? Possibly measure is the wrong word. Maybe the correct words are recognizing and attributing a contribution. Here are some thoughts:

- It would be possible to assess if a supplier has been innovative—for example, if a supplier proposes new solutions to needs, proactively, whereby the customer gets more capability for no additional cost, then the supplier is being innovative as well as proactive. This is definitive, so it can be recognized and fed back to the supplier.
- It might be possible to quantify the savings such an innovative solution delivers, and it might be possible, in this example, to get to a monetary value ROI. But not all innovation would automatically be so defined.
- Qualitative aspects of performance can be identified and sometimes quantifiably valued but trying to put in place a metric type KPI to measure such elements is not always possible or often not desirable.
- In conclusion, qualitative aspects of supplier performance can be identified/recognized, should be attributed to the supplier, but there does not have to be a hard measure applied to them.

### Thought Provokers

1. In your organization is there a multilevel supplier performance review process, with open communication to and from each level?
2. Are their planned reviews on an agreed frequency for all major suppliers?
3. Are the KPIs in contracts accepted as relevant for the duration of the contract or are they reviewed for relevance?
4. To what extent do you feel KPQs can be used to have conversations with suppliers where there is a performance shortfall and see green, feel red is being experienced?

## *Takeaways*

From a personal learning perspective, what are your three key takeaways from this chapter?

| | |
|---|---|
| 1 | |
| 2 | |
| 3 | |

# CHAPTER 12

# Operational Negotiation

*In this chapter: defining negotiation, the significance of negotiation in the lifecycle, the focus for operational negotiation, the different negotiation approaches, planning to negotiate, an outline structure for managing a negotiation meeting, behaviors to apply in reaching agreements*

## Defining Negotiation

The following two definitions of negotiation appear essentially the same, but there is an important difference in the sense and the context.

- Negotiation is the process of reaching an agreement that is acceptable to all parties.
- Negotiation is the process of reaching agreement from an initial position of no agreement.

The common theme is that negotiation is about reaching an agreement. The difference is that in the second definition there is an assumption that negotiation becomes necessary only if there is a difference of opinion on a matter, and so, a position of no agreement. In a sense they are both correct but being aware of the difference will help in understanding how other parties—in this case, the supplier—may view a negotiation. For example, if a supplier proposes a project plan and it is readily agreed to by the decision makers in the customer organization without any amendment, has there been a negotiation? Arguably not, as taking definition two, there has not been an initial position of no agreement.

In reality, the most common situation is that the supplier submits a proposal or a plan to the customer, this is discussed, and some aspects of the proposal will be readily agreed to; however, there will be some elements that cannot be accepted, so a meeting is required to discuss the issues, refine the proposal, and come to an agreement.

## The Significance of Negotiation in the Supplier Lifecycle

Why have I spent some time on the definition, tabling two versions and then qualifying the rationale for the two versions? The reason is that it is a key skill required for anybody involved in a supplier management role, and it is relevant in all stages of the supplier lifecycle. In these stages the negotiation will not always be with the supplier, but with colleagues and other internal stakeholders. For example:

- In the *Identify* stage it is likely that there will be some differences of opinion as to what the requirements definition document should cover, what the priorities are. Some negotiation will, therefore, be required between the internal stakeholders before a final set of requirements can be published.
- In the *Research* stage there could be discussions about how the supply market is to be positioned, which suppliers should be contacted for initial information, how meetings are to be set up, who should be involved, and consequently, which of those should be invited to submit proposals. These can be quite complex and detailed discussions, involving a number of stakeholders, and inevitably, there will be different views. Negotiation will be required.
- *Sourcing* is where contract negotiation will take place. An RFP is issued to selected suppliers; responses are received; the shortlist drawn up; detailed discussions, negotiations with the possible suppliers; and selection made subject to negotiation.
- *Integration,* the stage where implementation takes place, as the newly appointed supplier is introduced and the service delivery planning takes place. Depending on the situation, negotiation could involve how the handover from the old to the new supplier

takes place, or if the initiative involves a move from internal to external delivery, a different set of handover actions need to be discussed and agreed upon.

- Integration moves the lifecycle through to the *delivery* stage. For the duration of the contract, which could typically be three years, the task is to ensure services are delivered as per contract. Negotiation, across a range of topics, will be a frequent element in this ongoing relationship. My label for the negotiations that take place during delivery is *operational negotiation.*

While negotiation is in play throughout the lifecycle, the focus for this chapter is on operational negotiation—negotiating on a range of issues during the life of the contract. The principles and skills I will cover can, of course, be applied to other types of negotiation—for example, the formal contract negotiation itself during the sourcing stage, agreeing on the handover/transition plan at the integration stage.

What areas and subjects can operational negotiation in the delivery stage cover?

The short answer is, a vast range of topics, with internal stakeholders and the supplier, ranging from straightforward conversations that are not consciously thought of as negotiations through to discussions that are quite complex, and certainly require planning and preparation. Negotiations at the various levels are likely to be happening on an ongoing, daily basis. Here are some examples:

- Tasks for the supplier for the next week need to be reprioritized at short notice; this may cause the supplier some problems.
- The next review meeting, scheduled for two days' time, needs to be rescheduled—this will present challenges, but it is important that a new date is agreed upon quickly so a new date can be scheduled.
- The requirements of one of the biggest user groups has changed, and the supplier will be expected to respond to these changes quickly. This is not the first time urgent demands have been put on the supplier.
- The key measures of performance agreed during the contract were not correctly thought through so must be changed.

- There is a serious disconnect between what a key user group says it requires from the supplier and what the supplier says is possible.
- The supplier is not performing to the agreed upon KPIs; customer feedback has become very critical. The supplier refutes some of the user group claims.
- Every change request being put to the supplier gets the same response: "Out of scope; we will provide a costing for the additional work."
- The contract is being terminated in four months. It is vital that the service support is maintained to the required standard during that period. The supplier's attitude is negative, and there does not appear to be anything in the contract specifically about responsibilities during exit.
- The supplier is changing people in the delivery team with increased frequency without any prior notice. The contract does not specify they need to confer, but there is a sense that they are taking the customer for granted.
- The supplier has provided a quotation for what is agreed as extra work, outside the scope of the original contract. The price is much higher than expected, but there is a strong pressure to get the work actioned.

All of these situations will involve some form and level of negotiation to reach a conclusion. Negotiation is a key part of a supplier manager's role. How negotiations are approached in behavioral terms will influence the outcomes, and how quickly agreements can be reached. From the aforementioned examples it is clear that operational negotiations vary in terms of complexity, criticality, and formality.

## The Different Approaches to Negotiation

How people view what a negotiation is will influence how they approach a negotiation meeting. If we go back to the second of the two definitions I provided at the start of the chapter,-"Negotiation is the process of reaching agreement from an initial position of no agreement," people who accept this version may approach negotiation defensively as the negotiation is happening because there is a disagreement. At the extreme, they might even see it as a fight.

There are three possible approaches to take in a negotiation:

### Conflict

"I am determined to win at all costs." At the extreme, there is no negotiation.

### Compliant

"I need to give them what they want to reach an agreement."

### Balanced

Sometimes called *principled negotiation*: "I will work with them on reaching an agreement that we are both comfortable with."

Option three—balanced negotiation—is the most effective approach in most situations. The conflict approach can be seen to work in some situations. For example, a customer who is a large multinational and has a supplier that is a small local company, and the customer represents 80 percent of the supplier's turnover, could probably take a conflict approach and force the small company to agree to anything, purely on the basis of power and leverage. This approach could be seen to be effective in the short term. In the context of working with a strategic mission critical supplier, however, relationship is important. The conflict approach does not support building relationships. Could a customer ever be in a position to have to take a compliant approach in a negotiation with a supplier? It feels unlikely, unless the customer requires a product or service that only one supplier can provide, in which case there is a strong lock in. How a negotiation is approached is about behavior—I suggest the default is *balanced* unless there is a compelling reason to take a different approach. The behaviors described later in this chapter assume this approach.

## Negotiation Planning

### Planner Checklist

Considering the range of possible situations where operational negotiation is relevant, different levels of preparation and planning will be necessary. The following checklist is designed to ensure that you always go into negotiations prepared. This need not be time consuming and any time invested will result in more focused discussion, with better and quicker outcomes.

- **Know your optimum position:** This is generally straightforward as it is what you want the supplier to agree to without any negotiation.
- **Know your final position:** This is the least attractive solution that you are prepared to accept.
- **What do we believe the supplier will concede/agree to?** You can only have a view, but it should be an informed view.
- **What points may the supplier seek to negotiate for:** They will want to get something in return for anything they concede to you.
- **What are you prepared to offer?** This may enable the supplier to agree to your requests.
- **What might they be prepared to offer?** They may be able to provide something of value that influences your position on other points.

To put the application of this planner into context, if you are negotiating something very transactional and straightforward, such as agreeing on some minor changes in the monthly performance reporting format, then a very brief mental checklist through the planner before picking up the telephone to discuss the changes is all that is required. At the other level, if some significant change requests have been submitted and the supplier's response does not cover some points to your satisfaction and their proposed costs seem excessive, then a more in-depth plan is required. The key message: Invest in planning before you negotiate.

In addition to the planner checklist, there are additional factors to consider when putting your plan together.

### The Concept of Relative Values/Impacts

Different parties attach different values and importance to different topics. Something that the customer may feel is minor and of little value could be viewed as important and of high value by a supplier; likewise, the perception of impacts.

- *For example:* Being prepared to act as a reference site by providing a recommendation for a supplier could be seen as a minor point by the customer but of high value by the supplier. What is the cost to the customer of agreeing to such a supplier request? In monetary terms *nothing*, possibly a minor cost in terms of time. The potential value to the supplier of a reference from a current customer is high. The learning point: Think of the value of what you can offer to a supplier through their eyes.

- *For example:* The customer proposing a move from T+M (time and materials) to fixed price contracts could be seen as a major value to the customer, but possibly a major concern for a supplier, depending on the specific arrangements in the current contract. The learning point: View values and impacts from the supplier's perspective as well as your own.

### Best Option to Reaching an Agreement

A question that focuses the mind is, if, as the customer, I cannot reach an agreement with the supplier on this point, what is my best option? The answer to this will influence the negotiation stance.

- *For example:* If the conclusion is that to move to another supplier is not practical, in terms of cost, disruption, time, etc, there will be more pressure to reach an agreement with the current supplier. It is also useful to think through, what is the supplier's best alternative to reaching an agreement? Is it better to reach an agreement, although not on ideal terms with the current customer, or to find a new customer to replace the lost revenue? Which would involve the most time? Which would be represent more cost to the business? Learning point: Be clear about the final position and how acceptable that is, and see the situation from the supplier perspective as well.

In their groundbreaking book, *Getting to Yes,* on how to negotiate successfully, William Ury and Roger Fisher introduced the concept of the BATNA—best alternative to a negotiated agreement. Many years after publication it is still recognized as one of the most authoritative works on the art and science of negotiation.[1]

### The Concept of Leverage

Leverage is the ability to influence the other side to move closer to one's negotiating position. *Types of leverage include logic, positive, and negative leverage.*

- Logic leverage: Use facts and rationale to present the case. For example, if it can be demonstrated that the standard warranty periods in the industry are superior to those being offered, the request to the supplier to improve their warranty terms is based on accepted norms and market standards. Learning point: Support a request or demand with a reasoned case wherever possible; it is the type of leverage that is difficult for the supplier to challenge.
- Positive leverage: This is the ability to offer something the supplier finds of value. For example, informing the supplier that there are several new projects on the horizon, and if they can accommodate the change requests on the current work with no significant on cost, they will be in a better place when bidding for the future work. Learning point: Use only if there is a genuine possibility of additional work and emphasize that there is no guarantee.
- Negative leverage: This is the ability to penalize the supplier. For example, if the supplier will not agree to the performance improvement plan, then a formal escalation procedure can be instigated that could limit their ability to secure future business at least in the short term. Learning point: While a valid tactic, it must be applied with considered thought to avoid a perception of conflict negotiation being practiced.

The following *negotiation planner template* is (see Table 12.1) a practical tool that enables you to summarize the information you have

---

[1] R. Fisher, and W. Ury. 1981. *Getting to Yes*. Published by Penguin. ISBN 97801401 57352.

collected from the planning stage and present it in a logical, visual format. For relatively straightforward negotiation situations with a supplier, you can use it to study and refine your own thinking. For more complex topics, when you will be negotiating with colleagues, it can be applied as a team planning tool.

*Table 12.1 Negotiation planner—a practical checklist to enable systematic planning of key steps before engaging in a negotiation with a supplier*

### Our Items and Positions

| Item | Optimum | Final |
|------|---------|-------|
|      |         |       |

### Supplier Items and Positions (View/Perception Only)

| Item | Optimum | Final |
|------|---------|-------|
|      |         |       |

### Possible Concession Trades

| If they agreed to (our requests) | We could possibly agree to (their requests) | Values Us/them | Difficult L-M-H |
|----------------------------------|---------------------------------------------|----------------|-----------------|
| 1                                | 1                                           |                |                 |
| 2                                | 2                                           |                |                 |
| 3                                | 3                                           |                |                 |
| 4                                | 4                                           |                |                 |

### Our/Their Leverage Items

| Our leverage | Their leverage |
|--------------|----------------|
|              |                |

## Framework for Handling a Negotiation Discussion

This seven-point plan provides an overall framework for managing a negotiation discussion with a supplier. It can be applied to a range of situations regardless of the subject and complexity. It is important to differentiate between structure and formality. This plan can be applied to a formal meeting involving numerous attendees; it is equally relevant for informal one-on-one meetings conducted over a cup of coffee. Even informal meetings can and should be structured.

1. Agree on the issue.
2. Agree on the meeting outcome you both want.
3. Ask them what they are proposing.
4. Put your suggestions on the table.
5. Discuss and analyze the options.
6. Reach agreements.
7. Confirm what has been agreed upon.

To put some detail and context to each of the seven points in the template:

- Agree on the issue: This involves defining and agreeing on the item(s) that need to be discussed and resolved via a constructive negotiation. It is important that all outstanding points are stated at the outset. It is counterproductive to have reached agreements, when halfway through the meeting other issues are raised that could affect previous agreements.

- Agree on the meeting outcome you both want: This may sound obvious but getting clarity on what both parties' expectations are is important, as it will influence the discussions. For example, is the meeting about reaching agreement on all points? Is it about merely getting to understand the points and then adjourning to consult with colleagues before reconvening?

- Ask them what they are proposing: This sequencing is important. Get the supplier to state what they are proposing to resolve the outstanding points. The meeting has been prescheduled, so they should have thought through the options from their perspective. While negotiations should be balanced, with an objective of a win-win, if the supplier has revealed their thinking before the customer puts their ideas forward, the customer has an advantage. The supplier suggestions will provide some clues and ideas as to their overall thinking, what they see as being difficult, what they see as being relatively straightforward. In negotiation there is openness and openness. Information is power.

- Put your suggestions on the table: In the spirit of openness and collaboration it is important for the customer to then put their ideas forward. It is important to remember that by putting ideas forward you are not committing to them—at this stage they are ideas for discussion, which can be accepted or refined and accepted or rejected, taken off the table.

- Discuss and analyze the options: As both sets of ideas are now open this is the stage where the possibilities to reach agreements are discussed in detail. This can involve a trading process whereby if the customer agrees to something a supplier is requesting, then what can the supplier offer in response to a customer request or demand. Open behavior is key so that suggestions can be built and developed. Trust is important, because if the supplier is suspicious of the customer motives, this will restrict openness. While there is no hard and fast rule, the accepted wisdom is that it is a good idea to start off discussing what should be the *easy wins*—the areas that both parties can agree on without difficulty. If the most difficult item is first on the agenda, the risk is that you never get past it. If there are five items to discuss and four have been agreed upon, there is a greater motivation to work for an agreement on the final one, even if it is the most difficult.

- Reach agreements: The logical and positive outcome is that agreements can be reached regarding the way forward on resolving the problem, on a contract change, on fine-tuning the project scope, and so on.

- Confirm what has been agreed upon: Negotiations can be lengthy and potentially complex, involving a number of points that are interrelated. There are many examples of customers and suppliers walking away from a meeting believing there have been agreements, only to find out later that their expectations regarding future actions were quite different.

## Behaviors in Reaching Agreements

The following represent core negotiation behaviors and skills. It is unlikely that you will need to use all of them in one negotiation, so think of them as a menu you can select from when needed.

## Establish the Principle of Give and Take at the Outset

Working within a balanced negotiation framework, with an objective of win-win, the principle of give and take needs to be accepted by both parties. This is so fundamental that it could even be incorporated into the working code (see Chapter 8). A statement in the code could be, *when negotiating we will always take a balanced approach, and accept that negotiation is about give and take, to arrive at outcomes acceptable to both of us.*

## Ask Questions

It is not an obvious negotiation skill, but effective questioning of the supplier is vital. Answers to questions inform about the supplier's understanding of the issues, the degree to which they understand the customer requests, what ideas they have to provide solutions, what do they find difficult, what can they agree to relatively easily, what are their concerns, what are their constraints. Questions can also be used to commit: "Is this an idea you can accept? If not, what are your reservations?"

## Generate Options and Alternatives

If there is a binary choice of *yes/no* there is a risk of receiving a *no*. The more options there are, the more opportunities there are to reach an agreement. Therefore steps 3 to 5 in the meeting template are very important. Steps 3 and 4 generate the possible ideas, and step 5 is the discussing, refining process.

## Build Debt

Tactically, in a negotiation, a customer may decide to give a concession to a supplier; this could be something that has a high value to the supplier, but the cost of giving it is modest, therefore, easy. The concept of relative values and impacts covered earlier in this chapter provides the example of the customer being prepared to act as a reference site by providing a recommendation for a supplier. Building debt is making it clear to the supplier that if they are given a concession by the customer, it is being logged, and in the spirit of give and take, the customer will expect something in return.

This should not be stated in a conflict tone but displaying to the supplier that they are dealing with someone who is aware and commercially minded.

### Use Standards and Objective Criteria

Sometimes negotiation progress can be hindered by opinion and bias rather than fact. Whenever possible, therefore, substantiate a position with facts and data. For example, in a contract negotiation, payment terms become a point of discussion. To take an extreme example, purely to demonstrate the principle, a supplier states that their contractual terms state that payment should be received within 10 days of invoice date. The customer pays all invoices within 45 days. The industry standard is between 45 and 60 days. In such a negotiation the customer can use standards and objective criteria as a rationale for their payment terms. The customer could suggest to a supplier that in special circumstances they might be prepared to agree to special terms of 30 days, in the context of give and take, but 10 days would never be accepted.

### Ask for Assistance

This is a very open behavior, based on the adage "What can you do to help me help you." The supplier is making a request that is difficult for the supplier manager to agree to. This could be, for example, a request to revise the deadlines for completion of key milestones in the delivery of a major project. There are some genuine pressures on the supplier, so there is some sympathy, but the supplier manager feels that if they seek agreement from senior management for the change, there will be a clear *no*. So, asking how you can help me to help you in this example could be, "In isolation I think this is difficult, as I think my management will say no. What could you offer in return to help me get a positive decision for you?" This could be the supplier agreeing to increase resources during the final phase of the project, so end date is not impacted, even though some short-term timelines will be pushed back.

### Summarize Frequently

Summarizing is important for two reasons. First, it is a reminder of what has been agreed upon, and therefore, acts as a motivator to continue even if some of the discussion is now getting difficult. Second, it prevents misunderstanding about what has been agreed upon.

## Defer

There is a danger in any negotiation that the progress gets stalled because both parties become stuck on one point and the meeting descends into a repeated circular discussion. The risk is that no other points get discussed. Deciding to defer the item is a way of unlocking the impasse and being able to move on—provided, of course, that the difficult item is revisited.

## Adjourn

Adjourning is sometimes necessary—both parties may need to confer with colleagues in their respective organizations before final decisions can be made.

## Be Clear about the Nonnegotiables

This is a very important point, and one that needs to be positioned carefully. If certain items in a discussion are genuinely nonnegotiable, then it is fair to clearly state them. It is a signal of openness and makes the best use of time—it is pointless negotiating on a point that is fixed. It is worth making sure that something really is nonnegotiable before stating that it is. The reason is that if there are too many red lines and if some of them are incorrectly labeled as such, then there are two possible negative consequences—the negotiation becomes unnecessarily constrained and credibility is damaged. If a nonnegotiable suddenly becomes negotiable, then questions are raised about the negotiation tactics.

## When Saying No, Say Why

If the supplier receives a blunt *no* to their requests and suggestions, this gives the impression of an autocratic and conflict approach. Of course, it is valid and at times necessary to say *no* to a supplier. Taking the time to explain the reasons behind the refusal changes the sense of the message entirely. This is not advocating a soft option but is reiterating the importance of relationship with a supplier. The reasons for refusal could be numerous—company policy, legal, regulatory. Whenever possible be open about the reasons. It demonstrates that you as the customer have constraints that they will understand.

### Get behind the Stated Position to the Underlying Interests

In the planning template I stated that having optimum and final positions for all points in a negotiation is essential as by doing so the maximum and minimum objectives are being defined. There can be points in difficult negotiations when both parties keep restating their positions, neither is prepared to move from them, and eventually they probably stop listening to each other. If a supplier is refusing to move from their stated position, but the issue is important from the customer perspective, then the situation needs to be resolved but going around *our positions* in a circular discussion is not a solution. Asking questions to find out what is behind the stated position is a better way forward; it does require an open relationship and trust.

# Case study

The following case study represents a typical situation with a technology supplier working on a system enhancement project. After the brief explanation of the background there are some examples and guide points to show how some of the principles covered in this chapter can be applied to a supplier situation.

*The situation—scope change request*

As a supplier manager in the organization you are midway through a project that a supplier is delivering. At the last review meeting you discussed some system enhancements that are required on the basis of the changing needs of the business. It was agreed that the supplier would provide a costing. You see the work as minor and have estimated probably 12 to 14 man days. The costing guide they have provided is based on a minimum of 20 man days, possibly 25. You questioned this during a telephone conversation. The response was, "This is a realistic estimate." As a review is scheduled in the next few days, you agreed to pick up the discussion then.

This supplier has been working with the organization for the last 18 months and has been involved in a number of projects. The outcomes and the performance have been generally positive, and there are significant opportunities for them to bid for more work over the next couple of years.

The issue of them *over quoting* on scope change work has been raised before. They have pushed back saying that often the requirements are poorly defined so sizing the work has been difficult for them.

They are a reasonably niche supplier, and in the short term at least it makes sense for you to develop the relationship, and certainly, this is the view of your manager. There are, however, other players in the market, so you feel it would be sensible to look at these. For this particular piece of work, though, there is some urgency to get the required changes finalized and incorporated into the project plan. You, therefore, do need to reach an agreement at the meeting.

What questions could be put to the supplier to get a better understanding of how they arrived at their figure?

- Why is there a range of 20 to 25 man days in the costing estimate?
- What assumptions have you made in producing the estimate?
- Can we see a detail breakdown of specific tasks and times calculated?
- To what resource (in terms of level and experience) will you be allocating this work?
- When would you expect this additional work to be completed?

Potentially what are the solutions to closing the gap between your 12 and their 25 man day estimate?

- Ask the requesting business function to prioritize the additional requirements in terms of *must have* and *nice to have*. Can any of the requirements be taken out?
- Assuming the supplier 20 to 25 man day range builds in contingency for additional change, you can assure them that once the new work

is agreed upon, that specification will be frozen, so this derisks the situation for the supplier.

- Suggest that some of the customer IT resources could be allocated to the project for a period of time, thereby reducing the extra man hours the supplier needs to invest.
- A combination of the preceding suggestions potentially moves the gap from the supplier optimum of 25 man days and the customer 12 man days to the respective final positions of 20 and 14 man days. Some descoping of the change request and offering of resources potentially closes the six-day gap in final decisions.

What is your best alternative to reaching an agreement with them? What leverage does the customer have?

- In the short term there is no realistic alternative to agreeing with the supplier on the terms for actioning of the additional work.
- In the mid- and long term you have the positive leverage of more potential work for the supplier.
- In the mid- and long term you have the negative leverage of moving the work or some of the work to other suppliers who have a similar capability.

I emphasize that this is purely an example to illustrate how the principles can be applied. While every situation is unique, the broad planning principles, structure guides, and behaviors are a constant.

### Thought Provokers

1. In your experience, what negotiation approach do suppliers take when negotiating with your organization? Do you believe their approach works in your and their best interests?
2. To what extent do you feel that the possible constraints that suppliers have are considered when requests and demands are being put to them?
3. How viable is a conflict approach to negotiation in dealing with key suppliers? To what extent can it work? What are the risks?

4. Should a statement about an agreed approach to negotiation be incorporated into the working code?

### Takeaways

From a personal learning perspective, what are your three key takeaways from this chapter?

| | |
|---|---|
| 1 | |
| 2 | |
| 3 | |

# CHAPTER 13

# Managing Changing Requirements

*In this chapter: the likelihood and nature of change requests; the supplier manager role in managing the change request process; checklists of tasks and actions to reach agreements on the change; summary of skills required for managing the change process*

## The Likelihood and Nature of Change Requests

The range of services that strategic suppliers provide is broad and includes IT support services, IT infrastructure development, HR services, facilities management, customer services, back office business processes, marketing, security, components supply, logistics, telephony/communications, accountancy services, legal services, and consultancy. Given the range of services there are a number of different contracts and contract types; for example, specific project-based engagements, 3-to-5-year service delivery contracts, outsourcing and offshoring engagements, call-off schedules, time and materials arrangements, and framework agreements.

A range of products and services are thus being provided with an array of contract arrangements. A common thread running through all of them is that in the vast majority of cases the requirements that were originally defined, and against which the original proposals were submitted, and against which the contract was agreed, will most probably evolve and change during the duration of the contract. This is irrespective of how accurately and definitively the requirements were described at the outset—changing requirements are more the norm, rather than static requirements.

What is the nature of the change requests? Again, there is a broad spectrum, ranging from IT system functionality upgrading to performance reporting standards; from volumes of components on a monthly call-off to new call centre customer service standards; from new regulatory legislation for certain business processes to extending the scope of facilities management services.

Regardless of the products or services being supplied and of the change requests, the requests will not necessarily happen automatically. Some change requests will be relatively straightforward and can be actioned via a standard process; others will be more complex and could involve contract amendments.

## The Supplier Manager Role in the Change Request Process

The role of the supplier manager as a conduit between the supplier and the end customer was established in the introductory chapter; this role is particularly important in managing the change request and the resolution context. While specific roles will be dependent on organization structure and reporting lines, at a generic level, someone, and I specifically mean the "supplier manager," has the responsibility to receive a change request from a customer/stakeholder in the business, analyze it, relay it to the supplier, and broker an agreement as to how and when the change request is actioned. That very straightforward description hides what can be a difficult and convoluted process. The straightforward requests are easy to manage, so I shall not dwell on them, but instead focus on those that present a challenge.

What are the potential challenges?

- There is nothing in the contract that defines how change requests should be managed. Most contracts should have a section that defines the change control process, in which case the challenge is minimized, as there are a set of rules that can be applied. Hence, a key learning point is to know what is in the contract.
- The requirements in the contract are very tightly defined, and there is nothing that allows for responding to the changing needs of the

business. Of course, tightly defined requirements are necessary at the front end of the life cycle (the "identify" stage), but this should be balanced with some inbuilt flexibility, within parameters.

- A consequence of the first two points is that suppliers will declare changes are "out of scope," so any changes will require additional work, with subsequent costs.
- The flipside of the previous point is that the end users, the requesters of the change expect the supplier to respond to any change request regardless of the level of change and work involved.
- The change requests are not defined to the necessary detail, so suppliers are unable to accurately assess what is involved.

As a result, in a worst case scenario the supplier manager must manage a change request where there is no mechanism in the contract for change, where the change request is poorly defined, where the requester expects the supplier to respond without question, and where the supplier is inclined to treat any change as out of scope. While this scale of challenge is extreme, it is useful to have some clear guidance on how to manage the process.

The following charts provide a road map that defines the supplier manager role and the approach by which each of the steps involved can be effectively managed. The assumption in this sequence is that there is a change request from the business and this is communicated to the supplier manager, who acts as the bridge between the end user customer and the supplier and is responsible for reaching an agreement for the actioning of the request.

### Overview: Supplier Manager Role in the Change Process

1. On receipt of change request, clarify the requirements, the background to, and the context for the request with the business area concerned.
2. Submit change request to supplier in the agreed format defined in the change control process
3. Receive supplier response to the change request and talk with the business area. If the supplier proposal meets requirements (specification, quality, time, cost), then agree and sign it off.

4. If supplier response cannot be signed off (in/out scope disagreement, timescales, costs, etc.), then meet to discuss situation with supplier.

5. In parallel to the preceding steps, and after discussions with supplier, there is possibly a need to meet with the business area, which may include managing expectations.

6. Facilitate a meeting to negotiate an agreement that meets the business requirements and is supported and achievable by the supplier.

This is a high-level "thought map"—the details will be driven by the relationships and roles and responsibilities of the supplier manager and business area.

## Points to Cover with the Business Area Requesting the Change

Some change requests will be simple and straightforward, requiring no or little debate. In other situations, it will be necessary to push back on the business area if the requirements are not clear or if the validity of the request is in doubt. This checklist is based on a series of logical questions on which to base a discussion and gain clarity.

The checklist provides a structure, but what will define the effectiveness of these discussions is the behavior and the communication style that is used. The reality is that the supplier manager is perceived by the business area/end user as the supplier and them as the customer. The guidelines discussed in Chapter 10—supplier communication and influencing—can be equally applied to discussions with the customers. The "rule" of direct on the what (need to discuss your recent change request) and engage on the how (I need to ask questions to get a clear understanding of the requirement) is very effective. Also, operational negotiation, as covered in Chapter 12, will often be required in these and subsequent discussions.

- What are the drivers for the change request?
- What are the envisaged benefits to the business?
- Are these requirements agreed with all parties/stakeholders involved?

- Are these the definitive changes required in the foreseeable future?
- Is this initiative signed off in the business (subject to cost considerations)?
- In your view, is this change request in or out of scope given the parameters in the initial definition of requirements statement?
- If out of scope, is the budget available for the additional work?
- What is the budget?
- Have you prioritized items within the request on a "must have/nice to have" basis?
- What is the deadline for completion of the work?
- Implications for the business if the deadline cannot be met?
- What flexibility is there on completion date?
- In terms of importance, how does this request rate against other change requests already in the system?

The answers to these questions will provide the information to assess the request and decide the next steps. If the next step is to present it to the supplier and the supplier agrees, the actions for the change are scheduled, so the task is then simply to track the action through to completion, keeping the business area/end user informed of progress.

## Checklist: Points to Cover with the Supplier If Their Initial Response to the Change Request Is Not Accepted

What are the possible reasons for a supplier not to respond positively to a change request— "positively" implies agreeing to the request, delivered to requested time, delivered within existing budget to time with no impact on other priorities. Therefore, the possible reasons for not responding positively, and therefore not being accepted by the business area or the supplier manager, will be driven by concerns about scope, cost, time, and resources. The following checklist, also based on the questions to ask, will help in the discussion with the supplier.

*Questions to the supplier:*
- Can you talk me through your understanding of what the new requirements are and what you believe is involved?

- What is your rationale for seeing the change as being out of scope? (if the supplier manager and the business see it as in scope)
- Can you provide me with a detailed breakdown of the schedule and work involved, given your understanding of requirements?
- What are the constraints on your ability to deliver to the requested deadline?
- Linked to the preceding questions, what resources would you need to put in to meet the deadlines, and what costs would be involved?
- Looking at the existing change requests, are there any possibilities of achieving economies/time savings by combining some of the activities?
- Can we discuss possible opportunities to reprioritize the change requests currently in the system?
- What solutions do you suggest to enable us to move forward and action the change request?

It is important to approach these discussions with suppliers with an open mind. They could be right. They are closer to the detail of the work involved, so their understanding could be more accurate than that of the supplier manager or the business area involved.

## Checklist: Points to Cover with Requesting Business Area If the Supplier (Initial) Response Is Not Accepted

The discussion with the business area will, of course, depend on the outcome of the meeting with the supplier to establish why they see issues in actioning the change request. It could be that the supplier has made some suggestions that the business area will view positively, or there could still be outstanding issues that need to be resolved. The checklist below provides a range of the areas to discuss, the questions to ask, and the proposed actions to resolve the issue.

These discussions reinforce a key part of the supplier manager role that was highlighted in the introductory chapter—representing the business and the end users to the supplier and representing the supplier to the business and the end users. If the actioning of a change request is not straightforward, then pushback to the supplier and/or the business area, in positive terms, will be necessary.

The objective is to arrive at an agreed position to take back to the supplier.

- Provide feedback on the supplier's perspective and the logic of their response.
- If the supplier's analysis is valid, this needs to be explained.
- Manage expectations—if it is not possible to meet deadlines within the resources available, make this clear and explain why.
- Provide context—for example, the number of change orders being processed exceeds what was envisaged in the initial scoping of the work.
- Ask where the possible movement in requirements and priorities are. What is essential, and what is desirable though not necessary?
- Suggest looking at requests already in the system and see if any can be rescheduled.
- If in your considered view the request is out of scope, then make this clear, and discuss what further budget needs to be made available.
- Provide indicative costs obtained from the supplier.
- Agree the position to be taken when going back to the supplier.

## Arriving at the Desired Outcome

The obvious desired outcome is an agreed plan of action for the change request to be implemented; I have already covered the point that some change requests, hopefully the majority, are straightforward—the request is made, it is validated, it is passed to the supplier, the supplier responds with a solution that is accepted by the requester, change actioned.

The checklists in this chapter are designed to support the supplier manager in the situations that are not straightforward. The agreement in such cases may mean that the original request has been refined, priorities revised, budgets adjusted. The supplier will probably need to have demonstrated flexibility and responsiveness, reallocated resources at short notice, accepted some disruption to the work plan, and at times, within reason, shared some additional costs.

## What Is Required to Ensure Change Requests Are Managed Effectively?

I have already established that constantly evolving and changing requirements are the norm. In fact, if the business has requirements that are static, the supplier manager role is reasonably straightforward, as it is about ensuring that the supplier is performing in a very stable environment. Managing these changes is an important and potentially challenging part of the supplier manager role.

What needs to be in place, what skills are required to enable these situations to be managed effectively? First, a positive working relationship with the supplier and hence the importance of establishing a positive working code from the outset. Second, an understanding of the internal stakeholders and a recognition of their requirements. Third, an ability and a preparedness to challenge the internal stakeholders/business areas when required; for example, their change requests are not clear, they are expecting too much from the supplier, their priorities are changing daily. Fourth, the ability and preparedness to challenge the supplier; for example, they claim that the request is out of scope and represents additional work, while your view is that the request is reasonable and falls within the parameters of the deliverables as described in the contract. Finally, the ability to broker a negotiation—be it via a series of discreet supplier and then internal meetings, or combined supplier/internal business area meetings—in fact, these would be the most time effective, but the viability of this approach would depend on specific organization procedures.

### Thought Provokers

1. In your organization, do all contracts with suppliers have a specific section that specifies change control procedures?
2. To what extent do you feel that the business areas fully consider their changing requirements and take the time to define them clearly in a format that can readily be communicated to the supplier?
3. In your experience, how do suppliers respond to change requests—do they see it as, potentially, a conflict whereby they feel the customer is trying to get them to do more for less, or are they focused on responding positively to the customer requirements?

## *Takeaways*

From a personal learning perspective, what are your three key takeaways from this chapter?

| | |
|---|---|
| 1 | |
| 2 | |
| 3 | |

# CHAPTER 14

# Handling Conflicts and Disputes

*In this chapter: are disputes and conflicts inevitable? Responding versus reacting to conflicts, different conflict handling strategies, escalation and dispute resolution, case study*

## Are Conflicts and Disputes Inevitable?

"Inevitable" is too strong a word; "highly probable" is more accurate. Is even "highly probable" too pessimistic or a statement of reality? Let us consider the factors involved in a typical contract:

- The contract is likely to be for a 3-year period, possibly longer.
- Over that time the customer's needs and priorities will change, putting additional demands on the supplier, and some of them could be challenging.
- Given the strategic nature of the suppliers we are focusing on, the services they are delivering are likely to be complex.
- The implications for both the customer and the supplier of things not going well are considerable—for the customer, mission critical services and products not being delivered to standard, while for the supplier, reputational and financial risk.
- There are two sets of corporate interests involved.

Given the nature of the relationship that has been outlined, and the number of variables during the life of a contract, challenges and challenging conversations will be a feature. A combination of a good relationship, an established code of behavior, effective communication and influencing from both sides, the application of sound negotiation skills, and an established process for managing change will resolve most of these situations quickly and amicably. However, there will be occasions when positions become entrenched, there appear to be no easy answers, stress and pressure can impact behavior, the situation gets to stalemate. This is the area of conflict and dispute. The implications of unresolved conflicts are serious, so it is crucial to be able to resolve them to the satisfaction of both parties.

A contract will include a section on dispute resolution, and it is important for supplier managers to understand exactly what the contract states, as this will define a clear process, which will include what the escalation process is to resolve a dispute. However—and this is a key point—the best solution is to be able to resolve a conflict and a dispute *without* escalation. Continually pressing the escalation button potentially damages the relationship. The contract is there to protect both parties; it should not be seen as a tool to "threaten" the supplier. So, the message is clear—resolve the conflict/dispute at the operational level, and escalate only if it is absolutely necessary.

## Response versus Reaction Model

The response versus reaction model is a straightforward behavioral tool that provides clear guidance on how, in behavioral terms, to approach a conversation to resolve a conflict/dispute. A key aspect of the model is that while there is choice, there is one approach that will be the most effective in the vast majority of situations.

The principles that underpin the model are as follows:

- Response is considered, whereas reaction is immediate and knee-jerk. In managing conflicts, responding is far more effective than reacting.
- Reaction triggers one of two behaviors—*aggression,* which displays itself as *fight,* with the implication that someone will win and someone will lose. The second possibility is *nonaggression,* which displays itself as *flight.* This is about walking away, avoiding the discussion that is necessary if the conflict is to be resolved. Walking away merely postpones a resolution.

- The reactive behaviors tend to be emotional; this represents a risk as emotions can get in the way of a logical discussion.
- Effective response is dependent on *assertion*. Assertive behavior is factual and balanced and demonstrates the preparedness to protect one's position and interests, while recognizing the position and possible constraints of the other party. There is a direct link to principled or balanced negotiation, where the objective is to create a mutual win/win.
- When reacting, events are controlling you; when responding, you are controlling events.

The following diagram illustrates the reaction/response choice that is available and maps the steps involved in the response, considered mode. We are all human, and there will be times when, despite being aware of a model such as this, we react. Given that behavior breeds behavior, reaction will generate action from the other party, emotions build, and the chances of arriving at a solution to the problem that caused the original conflict are diminished. However, the good news is that at any time you can decide to switch to response; this will mean acknowledging that the initial reaction was a mistake—this is not a problem, as acknowledging you made a mistake is a sign of confidence, not weakness (Figure 14.1).

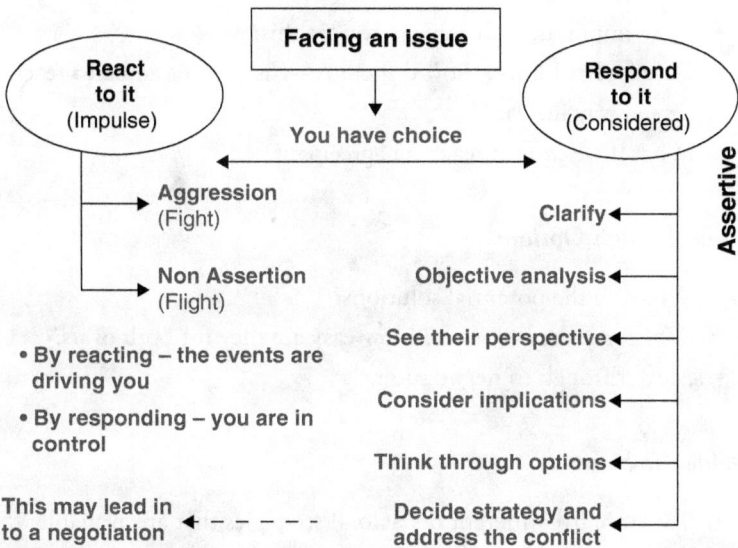

*Figure 14.1 Response versus reaction model*

## Clarify

- You may need more information to get a real understanding of the issue and what is behind it.
- Ask open questions, labeling why you are asking them, and clarify using closed questions and summary.

## Objective Analysis

- Now that we have more information, ask yourself the question—could the supplier be right?
- Have we been responsible in some way for this conflict?
- Has the additional information reinforced your initial views?
- Complete an objective summary.

## See Their Perspective

- Seeing their perspective may help you generate some solutions.
- It may enable you to understand some genuine concerns they could have.
- Seeing their perspective is different than agreeing with them.

## Consider Implications

- How important is it that we resolve this?
- Given what I know, how difficult/easy is it going to be to reach an agreed way forward?
- What if we cannot reach an agreement?

## Think through Options

- What are the potential solutions?
- Which are the best ones? How easy are they for both of us?
- Move through to negotiation.

## Decide the Strategy

- There are five different behavioral strategies that are available; they are explained next in this chapter.

- Of course, the other part of strategy is how to resolve the conflict in substance/material terms.

When these considered steps have been completed, moving through to addressing the conflict is possible; usually, reaching a solution will involve some negotiation. These steps may seem time consuming, especially if there is some urgency to resolving the conflict quickly and moving on. However, stepping back to reflect is a good investment of time. A reactive approach, involving heightened emotions, where a minor disagreement becomes a major row, will rarely result in a solution, and the necessary relationship repair work is very time consuming.

## The Range of Conflict Handling Strategies

Within the response approach, several possible strategies are applicable, depending on the specifics of the conflict that need to be resolved. Some conflicts will be easier to resolve than others; the level of difficulty/ease will be influenced by the importance of the issue, your ability to accept different ideas from the supplier, and, likewise, their preparedness to listen and accept other views. The situation will determine the degree to which you will need to *drive* (y axis) your position and case, balanced by your willingness to *engage* (x axis) with the supplier. "Drive" describes a tell/directive style, "Engage" a collaborative, working together style. These two dimensions lead to five possible strategies (Figure 14.2):

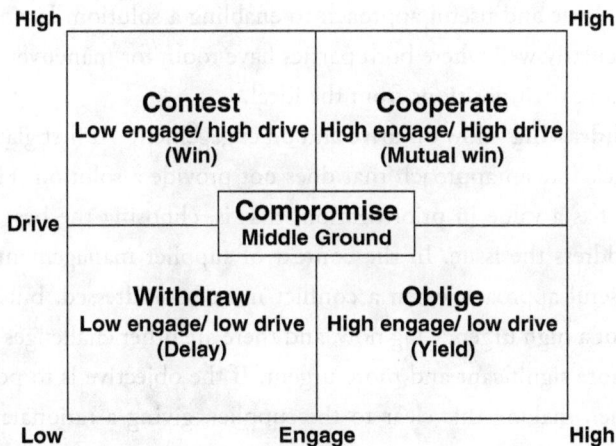

Figure 14.2 *Conflict handling strategies*

To provide some detail and context for applying in supplier management situations:

**Contesting**—high on drive, low on engagement. In the context of supplier management, this approach is appropriate if it is important to reach a resolution to the conflict, where there is some urgency, and where there is little or no room to negotiate with the supplier. It implies a win–lose outcome, so if overused can be seen negatively by a supplier and could, over time, damage relationships. However, it is necessary in some situations to protect commercial interests and service levels.

**Cooperating**—high on drive and high on engagement. In the context of supplier management, this should be the default approach, as the objective is to create a win-win, so it is closely aligned to balanced or principled negotiation, discussed in chapter twelve. In situations where reaching a solution is of equal and high importance to customer and supplier, and where there is confidence that a mutually agreeable solution is possible, cooperating is particularly relevant.

**Compromising**—midrange on drive and on engagement. In some eyes, compromise is sometimes viewed with a negative connotation. However, it is a very valid approach. In the context of supplier management, where relationships are important, the idea of give and take, while not ideal, is acceptable to both parties as a realistic and useful approach to enabling a solution. It works particularly well where both parties have room for maneuver and can move their positions from the ideal.

**Withdrawing**—low on drive and on engagement. At first glance, this feels like an approach that does not provide a solution. However, it has a value in prioritization, that is, choosing the best time to address the issue. In the context of supplier management, it is a useful approach when a conflict must be addressed, but there is not a high urgency tag now, and there are other challenges that are more significant and more urgent. If the objective is to postpone, then making this clear to the supplier, giving a rationale for the delay, is important. There is clearly a risk if there is a real conflict and the strategy is to avoid rather than delay—issues and problems generally do not go away, but tend to grow.

**Obliging**—Low on drive, high on engagement. This is the opposite of contesting, as obliging implies that you are prepared to lose and let the other party win. In the context of supplier management, this approach initially feels counterintuitive, on the basis that "customer is king." As discussed in previous chapters, strategic supplier relationships are characterized by a shared dependency, and relationships are important. In the chapter on negotiation, we discussed the concept of relative values and costs. For example, if, to resolve a dispute or a conflict, a concession from the customer costing the customer nothing or little but representing a high value to the supplier was discussed and agreed, then it would be a valid approach—solution agreed, relationship built, with a small "loss" to the customer. Of course, in future conflicts, the supplier would be more prepared to oblige, from the feeling that fair behavior should be reciprocated.

All the preceding five approaches are relevant and valid in the context of the response approach in the response versus reaction model. For example, withdrawing as a considered response is very different from flight in the reaction mode; likewise, contesting as a considered response is very different from fighting in the reaction mode.

Kenneth Thomas and Ralph Kilmann developed the "Conflict Mode Instrument," which is recognized as a leading analytical and behavioral model, to enable people to better understand their approach to resolving conflicts and to provide guidance to the optional approaches that are available in diverse situations. The concept is applied by organizations across many sectors, internationally. I recommend that you study their work.[1]

---

[1] K.W. Thomas. 1974. *Conflict Mode Instrument*. Tuxedo NY: Xicom. Publisher CPP. ISBN 13 978B0006SA349.

## Case Study

The following situation typically arises between a customer and a supplier. Read it from the position of a person in a supplier management role. The analysis following the description of the situation is designed to demonstrate how the conflict model and different strategies can be applied.

## The Situation

The supplier you are working with is new to your organization, and this is their first piece of work within the framework contract. Three months into the project there are issues. On submission of first phase deliverables, you have found several bugs and errors. From your perspective, the agreed QA procedures have not been adhered to. The fact that this is the second time this has happened on this project, and so early on, is a real concern.

You appreciate that they are on a learning curve with you, and you are prepared to be supportive. But their attitude is causing conflict. They are claiming that the requirements were poorly defined and that some of what has been requested since the start of the project are out of scope, and are stating that the timescales are now too tight. To address the issues that you have raised will mean extending the final delivery. You acknowledge that there have been some refining of requirements, but see it as being minor, and certainly in scope. You are under time pressure to deliver to the business.

## Analysis

What are the issues? Errors in the first phase deliverables, change requests disputed as to whether they are in scope or not, challenge to timelines originally agreed.

What approach is the supplier taking? Their approach is one of contesting. They are claiming that the change requests are out of original scope and that in the light of these demands the timelines originally agreed are now at risk. What approaches are open to you as the customer? It seems that the supplier is, intentionally or not, seeing the issues as one single thing, but the issues in fact are in some ways disconnected.

The errors in the first phase release are serious, and the QA procedures need to be questioned. On this specific point, the customer must take a cooperating stance initially to identify the reasons for the QA shortfalls, as the changing requirements could have been a contributory factor, albeit unlikely. If the supplier continues to push back, then the customer should move to contesting, as mistakes and quality issues are nonnegotiable and must be fixed. The change requests should be handled on a cooperative basis, as the in scope/out of scope nature is debatable until further information is gathered. The claim of risk to timelines by the supplier can be verified only after the nature and scale of the change requests have been agreed.

Is response or reaction most appropriate as a top line approach? There are numerous issues, and the most important behavior initially is to ask questions to understand more of the detail behind the reasons for the errors, the nature and validity of the change requests, and the impact on resources and timelines. A considered approach is key—even with a seemingly straightforward situation, the detail is potentially complex and challenging.

### Thought Provokers

1. To what extent do you feel a code of conduct that includes a point on "how we will handle conflicts and disagreements in a collaborative manner" would make difficult conversations easier?

2. Conflicts are often caused because the end customers do not always think through their requirements to the correct level of detail and expect suppliers to respond to conflicting and constantly changing requirements in unrealistic timescales. If this is so, what can someone in the supplier management role do to influence the end customer and other internal stakeholders?

3. In your experience, how knowledgeable are people in supplier management roles of the conflict and dispute resolution procedures that are included in the formal contracts that the organization has with all key suppliers?

4. Are conflicts necessarily negative? Can they be a catalyst for better future relationships?

## *Takeaways*

From a personal learning perspective, what are your three key takeaways from this chapter?

| 1 | |
|---|---|
| 2 | |
| 3 | |

# CHAPTER 15

# Keeping the Supplier Engaged

*In this chapter: the challenge of maintaining the supplier focus over the duration of the contract, the supplier state model, twenty action points to maintain focus*

## The Challenge of Maintaining the Supplier Focus

In chapter ten, supplier communication and influencing, I introduced the concept of the three phases of the relationship:

- **Start**—the initial period of the engagement covering integration and early stages of the deliver phase of the life cycle. Given, for example, a 3-year-engagement, the start phase would typically cover the first 3 months.
- **Stable**—After the initial settling in, the relationship should move to the stable state, which should be the default state for most of the contract period, and given a 3-year contract, the stable state would typically represent about 27 months.
- **Select/severance**—toward the end of a contract, a decision needs to be made with regard to the strategy for the future contract award. This could be as simple as re-engaging the current supplier for a further period (select) or, as is more likely, to return to the start of the life cycle and engage in a competitive tendering exercise. This may involve asking the current supplier to quote along with other suppliers, or, alternatively, for specific reasons they may be excluded. This is covered in more detail in chapter sixteen, Managing the Exit. In the 3-year contract example, this phase could involve the final 6 months.

It is a reasonable assumption that in the start phase the supplier will be positive, fully engaged, excited at the prospect of a new client and new contract, prepared to invest time to learn more about the organization, keen to impress and to build a positive relationship, and committed to perform to contract terms at the minimum.

The challenge for a supplier manager is to maintain the supplier's energy and enthusiasm at the same level as that demonstrated in the start phase for the total contract period. There is an argument that the contract is in place and it can be used to enforce satisfactory performance; however, in this chapter we are not discussing the contract, but the supplier state—how they feel about the client, how motivated they are to perform well.

Why should a supplier's commitment and enthusiasm change over time? There are a number of possible reasons—for example, the honeymoon effect wears off, the customer and the work are taken for granted, there are service level difficulties and challenges that were not envisaged, relationships can get damaged, newer customers receive more resource and airtime, the supplier realizes that the contract is more difficult and not as profitable as they thought, the exit period can bring additional risks. Although none of these risks are inevitable, the supplier manager needs to be aware of them, because the effect of such risks, should they materialize, will be a reduction in performance against the contract. To state the obvious, a key responsibility of a supplier manager is to ensure that the supplier performs to the agreed service standards, at the minimum, for the duration of the contract.

There is no magic solution to ensure that the supplier focus and enthusiasm will be maintained. However, there are actions that can be taken to minimize the risks, and in the rest of this chapter I will introduce

- The supplier state model—a tool that will help identify where a supplier is on a commitment and energy scale.
- A checklist of actions that can be taken on an ongoing basis that will support the objective of keeping the relationship (and therefore the performance) at the optimum level. These actions can be taken proactively, as part of planned actions, or reactively if, as a supplier manager, you are unlucky enough to inherit a damaged relationship and you must press the reset button. Taking actions proactively is more effective and easier than being in reactive mode.

It is worth noting that the customer can be as guilty as the supplier of losing focus and enthusiasm. If, for example, the customer repeatedly cancels review meetings because of other priorities, this sends a signal to the supplier. The saying "behavior breeds behavior" is very true and relevant.

## The Supplier State Model

The purpose of the model is to enable the supplier manager to assess the state of a supplier on the basis of their performance and a range of observable behaviors. It is intended as a guide to assist decision making.

There are two dimensions to the model, but the following dictionary definitions need to be addressed before I relate them specifically to the supplier context.

Energy—capacity for work, activity and completing tasks, exerting effort, ability to act.

Attitude—a way of thinking and feeling about something. A positive attitude demonstrates a willingness, a preparedness to try things, thinking optimistically. A negative attitude demonstrates a lack of cooperation, and nonconstructive behavior.

Those definitions could be debated and refined for a long time, but I think the overall message is clear. Now to relate them to the supplier state model.

There are four positions in the supplier state model:

- **Engaged**—high energy/positive attitude
- **Complacent**—low energy/positive attitude
- **Cynical**—high energy/negative attitude
- **Disengaged**—low energy/negative attitude

The objective is to keep the supplier in the high energy/positive attitude state for the duration of the contract. This is the state where performance will be optimal and the relationship most positive.

This is a key point—*it is unlikely that a supplier makes a conscious decision to become complacent with a customer*. It is not a deliberate act, but something that can happen over time. Given this assumption, the attitude will still be positive, but the energy level will have dropped off from that experienced previously. The implications are that performance will deteriorate over time, and the customer will feel that requests are handled less responsively. This will result in more difficult conversations at review meetings, possible institution of escalation procedures, diminishing levels of trust, and a more formal and contractual feel to the relationship.

If the supplier moves to the cynical state, then the energy/response level may be seen to improve because the supplier now sees risk to the contract and future revenues. So as a short term measure, they demonstrate a positive change; however, the attitude to the customer and to the relationship is now, on balance, negative. The motives are therefore selfish and defensive with the overriding aim of protecting short-term interests.

A situation where the supplier is in the disengaged state is clearly serious and may be difficult to resolve. Performance will have dropped off significantly, and the negative attitude is likely to have impacted relationships. The conversations become focused on poor performance and problems; the supplier manager will be facing pressures from end customers and other internal stakeholders to act.

It is important to emphasize that the journey from engaged to disengaged is not preordained. In fact, with skillful supplier management, any move from the high energy/positive attitude position can be prevented. The value of the model is that it demonstrates quite clearly what can happen and the consequent risks.

### What Are the Typical Behaviors for Each of the States?

#### Engaged

High capacity for work and achieving output; responds positively to requests, ideas, and challenges; is proactive in proposing news ways of working. Engaged suppliers are committed.

#### Complacent

At best, middling levels of capacity for work and output. They generally respond well to requests and ideas but need chasing to provide answers.

Little evidence of proactive thinking. Complacent suppliers are unconcerned and see no need to improve or change.

## Cynical

Display capacity for work and achieving output, but very selfish motivations; proactive ideas driven by selfish motives; generally skeptical about customer's motives and drivers; negative response to requests and ideas unless their purpose is served.

## Disengaged

Display low capacity for work and output; respond negatively to requests and ideas; no proactive or innovative activity; disengaged suppliers are uncommitted; performance is poor or at risk.

In the light of the dimensions and descriptions of behavior for each of the four states, it is an interesting exercise to carry out an "audit" of the state of suppliers you have responsibility for managing. As with all behavioral analyses, it is useful to think of tendencies and spectrums rather than absolutes—for example, a supplier in the complacent category would be demonstrating less energy than an engaged supplier, but it may not be low on an absolute scale. Supplier performance data, which is definitive, can be used in conjunction with the behavioral observations (Figure 15.1).

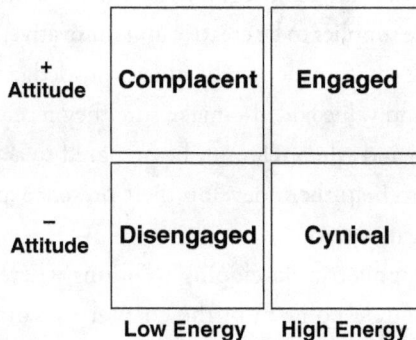

|  | Low Energy | High Energy |
|---|---|---|
| **+** **Attitude** | Complacent | Engaged |
| **−** **Attitude** | Disengaged | Cynical |

*Figure 15.1 Supplier state model*

### Twenty Action Points to Maintain Focus

The objective is to ensure that the supplier state is in the engaged box for the duration of the contract; As I have previously stated, it is reasonable to assume that the supplier will be engaged at the start of the engagement. The supplier manager's task is therefore to take actions to ensure that they stay there or, if they have moved into one of the other states, to take remedial action to return them to a high energy/positive attitude. The following actions represent what constitutes good practice, and many of them have already been described in other chapters, so the list serves as a summary checklist. At the start of this chapter, I stated that there is no single magic answer; therefore, the solution comes from selecting the most relevant action items for a specific supplier situation, applying them, and reviewing regularly.

1. Ensure that a code of practice has been put in place at the start of the engagement; review it regularly, update, and amend as the relationship develops.
2. Provide balanced feedback informally and as part of the performance review process. Often suppliers feel they only get feedback when there is a problem. Creating the balance is important.
3. Reinforce the service level agreement and key performance indicators (KPIs) at all reviews, as a positive reminder of the service requirements, and the ongoing performance against them.
4. Share information, specifically updates in the business, on how the strategy is developing. This provides the supplier with a context for how their services are an integral part of the customer business.
5. Encourage the supplier to be creative and innovative; provide feedback on the ideas, even if not actioned; and acknowledge when suggestions are adopted and value added—make sure they receive the credit.
6. When earned and when relevant, be prepared to act as a sponsor for the supplier to help them develop their presence and opportunities across the organization.
7. Involve the supplier in developing solutions wherever possible. Remember the guide point from the chapter on communicating and influencing—"direct on the what, engage on the how."

8. Review KPIs frequently to ensure that they stay aligned with changing business requirements and priorities.

9. Establish the principle that the specific performance measures, be they KPIs or project deliverables, represent the minimum expected levels of performance. This will encourage a working culture of continuous improvement.

10. Stay committed to review meeting frequency—cancellations signal to the supplier that you, the customer, are losing focus.

11. Ensure that review meetings are dynamic and interesting and do not just rely on a standard agenda—vary they venue, have specific agenda items, invite internal stakeholders, avoid sameness.

12. Provide a sense of belonging—give new supplier team members the same level of induction and orientation to the business as that given to the original team during the integration phase of the life cycle.

13. Create the opportunity to step back from the day-to-day business so that the broader relationship can be discussed, and plans made.

14. Be aware that customers can lose focus and become complacent about the relationship.

15. Give rewards for overperformance as well as service credits for underperformance. Also remember that reward does not always need to have a monetary value.

16. Make sure that reviews balance reviewing the past with learning for the future.

17. Ongoing positive challenge—ask questions, involve, discuss, engage.

18. Make sure feedback is genuinely two way—more than suppliers having the option of providing feedback to the customer, it is expected of them.

19. Be prepared to represent the supplier to internal stakeholders. In the introductory chapter the supplier manager's representational role was established as a key part of his or her function.

20. For remote communications, pay even more attention to the working code and communication forums. This point was covered in detail in chapter nine, cross-cultural working.

## Thought Provokers

1. From your experience, do you believe there is a risk that customers engage suppliers and assume that they will get on and deliver the required services for the duration of the contract because they are being paid to do so? Is it a valid view, or is it a mistake to believe that their energy and commitment will stay at the start level for 3 years? Over time?

2. Should suppliers of mission critical services be welcomed into the business and be encouraged to see themselves as part of the internal team? Or should they be kept at arm's length?

3. In your opinion, what are the major reasons for suppliers to become less energized and committed over time?

## Takeaways

From a personal learning perspective, what are your three key takeaways from this chapter?

| | |
|---|---|
| 1 | |
| 2 | |
| 3 | |

# CHAPTER 16

# Managing the Exit

*In this chapter: positioning—the end of the lifecycle, potential risks, possible situations moving into the exit phase, exit planner*

## Positioning—End of the Lifecycle and Potential Risks

For clarity, the context for the term *managing the exit* is very specific: ending of the current contract. This does not necessarily mean that the relationship with the supplier has ended, as, for example, the outcome could be that the same supplier is reengaged for a further period on a new contract. Alternatively, it could involve the termination of the relationship with the current supplier. There are a range of possible exit situations, and these are explained fully later in this chapter.

To position the exit phase in the context of the five-stage supplier lifecycle, it is important to note there are two distinct links:

- The termination period of the current contract is in the *deliver* stage because the delivery of the service must be maintained during the notice period to the end date.
- A parallel activity will be the replacement of the current contract with a new one, and possibly the current supplier with a new one. This takes us back to the start of the lifecycle; if the supply market has not changed, and if requirements are broadly the same as when the last engagement, then going straight to the *sourcing* phase may be possible. If there have been changes in either the market or requirements, then going to step one of the lifecycle—*Identification* of needs—followed by the *research* phases will be necessary. In fact, unless there is a compelling reason not to, I would always recommend following the entire lifecycle for all engagement activities.

This chapter focuses on managing the termination period, and the exit itself. For guidance on managing the parallel activity of going out to the market, and effectively starting another lifecycle journey, go back to the start of the book.

## Risk

Any change involves a certain amount of risk, the degree of which will be determined by the specific situation. For example, if the contract is being terminated and the supplier is not invited to bid for the future contract, there is bigger risk than if the supplier is being asked to participate in the new bid process. A key element of the exit planning template covered in this chapter is about risk identification and management. To be clear, risk in the context of the exit period is the risk to continued service/product delivery to the standards defined in the contract during the period from notification of termination to actual end date of the contract.

The exit plan must also consider the risks in the context of the nature of the service being delivered assessed in terms of mission criticality and strategic importance. For example, if there was risk to standard stationary supplies during an exit period, this would result in less of a red flag than if there was risk to key components supply for the production line, with the reality of production tending to stop if supply was interrupted.

## Possible Situations Surrounding the Exit

Understanding the reasons for the exit, and what the plan moving forward is, will be key inputs into the exit plan. The list described below covers the most common situations:

- The contract is ending, and the current supplier has not been invited to submit a proposal as part of the new bidding process.
- The contract is ending, and the current supplier was invited to bid for new contract but was unsuccessful.
- The contract is ending, and the current supplier has been invited to submit a proposal as part of the new bidding process and has been successful/likely to be successful.

- The contract is ending, and the current supplier does not want to be considered for the new contract.
- Premature ending of contract due to issues with supplier performance.
- No future requirement for the service.
- Service provision being taken in house.

In conclusion, there are a range of reasons for exit, and as is clear from the list above there are different levels of risk; for example, early termination due to poor supplier performance carries a greater degree of risk than a situation where the current supplier has been asked to retender, and because of relationship and past track record there is a high possibility of their securing the contract.

## The Exit Planner

The nine-point exit planner is a tool to guide and assist in the design of a comprehensive plan to ensure a smooth exit and transition to the new service/product delivery arrangement.

As a first step, a vital input for the exit plan is to refer to the original contract to determine what is included specifically *for continued service, roles, and responsibilities during the contract termination phase.* The more detail there is in the contract to cover this eventuality the better. A risk-free exit will require a good working relationship, but a contractual commitment will be helpful if reinforcement is required. I recommend you consult the contract owner—often someone in the sourcing team—for advice on this if the contract is unclear.

The nine points in the plan are not necessarily linear and sequential. Some action points can be, in fact need to be, in parallel.

### Nine Steps in Summary

1. Ensure you have an agreed exit plan with all the internal stakeholders.
2. Agree new supplier's involvement in the exit/transition plan.
3. Assess the risks and produce risk management plan.
4. Analyze the relationship for opportunities/issues.
5. Assess your leverage.

6. Conduct exit plan meeting with the supplier to agree plan.

7. Throughout exit, balance contract [what] and relationship [how].

8. Set up COMNET with all stakeholders.

9. Balance the "definitive plan" with being responsive to change.

Below is a breakdown and explanation of each point, listing all required activities:

1. **Ensure you have an agreed exit plan with all the internal stakeholders**
   - Stakeholders—procurement, legal, risk, business/customers and so on.
   - Check if all parties know what provisions are in the contract to ensure service continuity during exit.
   - Get inputs on possible risks during exit.
   - Discuss/agree strategy for service credits/debits and possible incentive plan; incentive can be an expedient approach during exit.
   - Get agreement on overall plan, including timelines, accountabilities, roles, and so forth.

2. **Agree new supplier's involvement in the exit/transition plan**
   - New supplier could be external or internal (if the service is being in sourced).
   - Their role in transition should have been made clear/agreed during procurement so this is now about refining and detailing.
   - Be as open in briefing them on current situation, relationships, and risks as possible.
   - Get their views/inputs on risks.
   - Brief them on any other external suppliers/services they impact or may impact them, brief them on the dependencies, and arrange for them to meet.

3. **Assess the risks and produce risk management plan**
   - From meetings with internal stakeholders and the new supplier, risks will have been identified.
   - These risks now need to be analyzed and risk management plans put in place, using risk management processes that are current in the organization.
   - Risks are factored into the exit/transition plan.

4. **Analyze the relationship for opportunities/issues**
   - The state of the relationship will be influenced by the background to the exit.
   - Over the course of the contract, how has the relationship been developed?
   - What good will exists and how can this help mitigate risk?
   - Have you built up some "credits" in the relationship bank that you can cash in if required?
   - Understanding the supplier's perspective and demonstrating your understanding can be positive.

5. **Assess your leverage**
   - At the end of the contract, when the supplier will no longer be sending you invoices, you will become an ex-customer.
   - But you still have leverage; you need to assess what this is and use it if required.
   - The most obvious point is that you are still paying them until the end of the contract.
   - On a broader basis, what other contracts do they still have in the organization? Are there opportunities for them in the future? How important is it for them to be able to quote you as a former customer? Would you be a reference site? What are the reputation impacts for them in not delivering during exit with you?

6. **Conduct exit plan meeting with the supplier to agree plan**
   - Summarize outputs/agreements from your meetings with internal stakeholders and new suppliers.
   - Present the draft exit plan, get supplier inputs, and refine as required.
   - Get their views in risk and factor these into the risk management plan.
   - Link the exit to the transitioning in activities and gain commitment on collaborative working with the new supplier.
   - Agree review processes, frequency, and the like.

7. **Throughout exit, balance contract [what] and relationship [how]**
   - This links back to working relationships discussed in other sections of the workshop.
   - Key themes have been (1) balance working to contract and relationship and (2) being directive on the what but engaging on the how.

- Depending on the reason for exit and the state of the relationship you may have to move more toward directive and micromanagement to establish more control in managing risks.

8. **Set up COMNET with all stakeholders**
   - Effective communication is important in all phases of the supplier relationship/lifecycle.
   - To minimize risks and to ensure a smooth transition, give communication an extra focus.
   - The COMNET defines who the stakeholders are, who needs to be communicating what to who (think of senders and receivers), in what frequency, and in what format/medium.
   - The COMNET should be in place anyway; during exit there is a possible need to formalize and manage more tightly to minimize any risk.

9. **Balance the "definitive plan" with being responsive to change**
   - An exit plan is essential to ensure a risk-free exit and transition.
   - However, situations can change during an exit—for example, there could be risks and constraints that were not identified earlier and that may impact schedules.
   - Changes and issues are not always caused by the supplier.
   - You may require the supplier to be responsive and flexible—therefore, within boundaries, be prepared to demonstrate this yourself.
   - Be very clear on the nonnegotiables.
   - Use reviews to reassess/fine-tune the exit plan as required.

## *Thought Provokers*

1. To what extent do you feel the exit phase of an engagement is sufficiently detailed to ensure all risks are identified and mitigation plans are put in place?
2. The principle of managing on a balance of contract and relationship is a key theme established in the opening chapter. During the exit phase do you believe that this balance may have to change? If so, in what direction?
3. For some contracts where the products or services have low strategic impact and where there are a number of suppliers in the market, is

it time effective just to renew with the current supplier if they have been performing well for the last 3 years? It could save a lot of procurement and operational management time.

## Takeaways

From a personal learning perspective, what are your three key takeaways from this chapter?

| | |
|---|---|
| 1 | |
| 2 | |
| 3 | |

# CHAPTER 17

# Summary, Key Messages, Summary of Reading List, and Other Resources

## Overarching Key Messages

- A clear and understood contract is required for effective supplier management. It provides the factual basis for the business relationship.
- However, relationship is equally important as the contract. Effective supplier management is about balancing managing on the contract and relationship in equal measure.
- There is a clear link between a good relationship, based on trust and fairness, and good supplier performance.
- People in a supplier management role—accepting that a generic job description does not exist—have a representational role, representing the customer to the supplier and vice versa.
- Managing the internal stakeholder relationships is as important as, and sometimes can be more challenging than, managing the supplier relationship.

## The Lifecycle—Overview

- There are five stages in the lifecycle that cover the end-to-end process of identifying, engaging, working with, and eventually exiting a supplier.
- The IRSID lifecycle model consists of the following steps: identify, research, source, integrate, and deliver.

- The lifecycle model provides a useful guide but can only be as effective as the effectiveness of its application. There must be communication and links from stage to stage, to prevent the real danger that each step is completed in isolation, with a silo-like mentality.
- Stakeholder management and communication is vital throughout all stages, particularly because the stakeholders can change as the lifecycle progresses.
- Communication, influence, and relationship management skills are required throughout all stages.

*(Reference Chapter 2)*

## Lifecycle—Identify (Requirements)

- The requirements identification stage is vital. If this is not concise, correct, comprehensive, and understood by all stakeholders, then the subsequent lifecycle stages will be difficult and have risk. It potentially means that the suppliers are provided with incorrect requirements, their proposals reflect those incorrect requirements, suppliers are engaged on a contract that is incorrect, etc. This point demonstrates how interconnected and interdependent the stages are.
- Involving the right people in defining and agreeing the requirements is a prerequisite and the start of identifying the right stakeholders, which is necessary throughout the lifecycle.
- The seven-point template for requirements identification provides a structure to work with. The seven points are executive summary, background and context, business requirements and drivers, scope definition, minimum performance standards, assumptions, and constraints.

*(Reference Chapter 3)*

## Lifecycle—Research

- Research is a key phase and is often not given enough attention or time because of pressures to find and engage with a supplier as quickly as possible once requirements have been defined. If possible, research should be carried out proactively independent of a live sourcing initiative. For example, if the area is facilities management is it practical to build knowledge of the market, possible suppliers, latest trends, and so forth in facilities via proactive research so it is available when required?

- There are numerous sources of information, both internal to the organization and external. Internal sources include procurement, finance, legal, risk, compliance, user groups, and subject-matter experts. External sources include current suppliers, potential suppliers, professional bodies, seminars, and exhibitions.
- As with data sources, there are potentially numerous influencing factors to be considered, such as technology development, regulatory, and socioeconomic.
- Understanding the supply market for the services/products to be sourced is a key factor in determining the sourcing as well as the overall supplier management strategy.

*(Reference Chapter 4)*

## Lifecycle—Sourcing

- The level of resource put into a sourcing activity will be driven by the monetary value of the products/services being purchased and the significance of them to the organization.
- There are several different sourcing models/approaches, but at a generic level there is a Request for Information (RFI), which asks potential suppliers for enough information for a screening in/out process to take place. Screened-in potential suppliers are then asked to submit a formal detailed proposal: Request for Proposal (RFP).
- Typically, an RFI consists of a request for a company overview, provides a very broad description of requirements, and provides guidelines for response.
- The RFP typically involves sections on statements of requirements, instructions for completing the RFP response, details of response formatting and content, how to respond to service, reporting, costing, and commercial requirements.

- The RFP also details for potential suppliers what the selection criteria are and how selection decisions are made.

*(Reference Chapter 5)*

## Lifecycle—Integration and Delivery

After sourcing, the selected supplier is now hired by the organization, so all subsequent activities become part of either integration or delivery stages or both.

### Contract and Supplier Background

As the contract has just been agreed, all the contract and supplier information should be known; however, is it necessarily known to the people who are now taking over responsibility for the operational management of the project or service delivery? This activity will be largely in the integration stage because it involves handover of information to the delivery team.

- Contract knowledge—what the supplier is contracted to deliver, to what standards, and to what price? In addition, what pricing methodology is being used, what are the key performance indicators (KPIs), how is performance measured and by whom and to what frequency? What is the review mechanism, what is the format of review meetings, what is the escalation procedure, and what is built into the contract to cater for scope change?
- Supplier background—how significant the supplier is to the organization, what other projects are they involved in, what were the selection criteria, how did they score on those criteria, do they have a track record in the organization on other engagements, and what was their performance like?
- Supplier and customer segmentation—how does the customer categorize the supplier, how does the supplier categorize the customer, what is the level of commonality of view, and how can the relationship be optimized?

*(Reference Chapter 6)*

*Internal Stakeholders*

- Knowing and being able to manage the internal stakeholders, as discussed earlier, is important throughout the lifecycle; however, the context here is managing the internal stakeholders after sourcing; these are the stakeholders with an active interest in the service or project delivery and therefore relevant through the delivery stage.
- Internal stakeholders can be put into one of the following categories—contract owners, subject-matter experts, specialist functions, business sponsors, and user groups.
- The RACI and INFORM models are both useful in identifying interests, roles, and responsibilities.
- Communication is an essential element in stakeholder management, and the COMNET provides a practical tool to ensure effective and timely communication.

*(Reference Chapter 7)*


*Establishing the Working Code*

- There will already be a relationship with the supplier, developed during the sourcing phase; however, as part of the integration phase, and to be maintained throughout delivery, the working code is an important element in achieving a positive working relationship.
- The working code describes a set of statements driven by the mutual expectations of behavior toward each other. It is important that the code is jointly developed, by you and the supplier, at the working team, operational level.
- The code should not include procedural items and should not form part of the formal contract. It should be viewed as an emotional contract.

*(Reference Chapter 8)*


*Cross-Cultural Working*

- Relevant when there is an offshoring supplier relationship whereby different national cultures are involved. In a sense, it is about the working code with a multicultural dimension.

- Often in offshoring relationships, the competence of the supplier is not in question, but rather the cultural differences, resulting in different expectations.
- Hofstede's six cultural dimensions provide insights into the possible cultural differences and how this can impact expectations, communication, and therefore relationships.
- In addition, the low-/high-context communication styles provide awareness of how different cultures communicate on the low/high, direct/indirect dimensions.

*(Reference Chapter 9)*

### Supplier Communication and Influencing

- The ability to communicate with, and influence the supplier, is fundamental to a positive and effective working relationship.
- During the course of a contract, there will be numerous conversations on a daily basis that require resolution to ensure service delivery is maintained. How those conversations are approached, in behavioral terms, will have a profound influence on the outcome.
- There is no single communication style for all situations—the approach to take will be driven by a range of factors. One of those factors could be the maturity of the relationship and the phase of the engagement—start, stable, severe/(re)select.
- The communication model shows a range of approaches on the basis of levels of direction versus levels of engagement.
- The suggested default, the most effective approach in most situations, is to direct on the "what" and engage on the "how."
- A massive benefit of engaging rather than directing is that you can use the supplier energy and their expertise.

*(Reference Chapter 10)*

### Performance Review and Development

- Frequent and planned supplier reviews are the prime activities to ensure sound governance.

- For a strategic supplier, reviews need to be at three levels—strategic, business, and operational. Each level should report outcomes of meetings to people involved at other review levels with that supplier.
- Typically, operational meetings should be monthly, business levels quarterly, and strategic annual. These are notional, and frequencies will be driven by the factors in specific relationships.
- Meetings are an opportunity to review performance, address shortfalls, and put in place remedial action plans.
- Reviewing the past should be balanced with looking to the future and into how performance and the relationship can develop.
- The KPIs established at the start of the contract should be reviewed regularly using KPQs.
- The hard measures of supplier performance, quite correctly, are the focus for determining the effectiveness of a supplier. However, reviews should also leave room to discuss the qualitative, value-added elements of the supplier contribution.

*(Reference Chapter 11)*

### Operational Negotiation

- Negotiation is involved in all phases of the supplier engagement; in the delivery phase, operational negotiation is in play on an ongoing basis to reach agreements on a range of areas necessary for the continued delivery of the services as per contract.
- Of the three approaches to negotiation, namely, conflict, compliance, and balanced, the most effective in most situations is balanced.
- Planning is key to effective negotiation—even for the simplest, least formal situation, it is good practice to use the planner checklist; for more complex situations, formal planning is necessary.
- In addition to the planner checklist, there are three specific factors to consider—relative values, best alternatives to an agreement, and leverage.
- The seven-point plan for running a negotiation meeting can be applied to all situations, regardless of complexity.

- Although having a structure and a plan is important, ultimately agreements are reached by the application of a number of positive negotiation behaviors.

*(Reference Chapter 12)*

## Managing Changing Requirements

- No matter how well the requirements are defined, or how aligned the supplier proposal is to those needs, the one for sure is that over the period of the engagement, needs will evolve and change. The supplier will be expected to respond to these changes.
- The contract will have a section on the change control process and how change orders are approved and actioned.
- The supplier manager conduit role between the supplier and the end users/other internal stakeholders as has been highlighted before, and it is particularly important and relevant in the change process.
- The templates contained in Chapter 13 cover the range of situations that are possible and need to be managed.
- Some requests are straightforward—forwarded to supplier, and deemed within scope by the supplier, they have the capacity to accommodate, and so can be agreed and actioned quickly.
- The most challenging requests are those that are not well defined, those that have nebulous business justification, those in which the supplier claims the request is outside the scope of the original contract, and those in which there are numerous other change requests in the system so as to warrant prioritization. These are the situations that challenge the supplier manager in the mediator role and call for a high level of negotiation skill.

*(Reference Chapter 13)*

## Handling Disputes and Conflicts

- Conflicts and disputes are not inevitable; however, realistically during a contract there will be disagreements between the supplier and the customer. They will need to be resolved quickly.

- The contract will include the escalation process for dispute resolution. However, wherever possible, the dispute should be managed at the operational level without pressing the escalation button. This approach makes best use of time and supports the development of a positive relationship.
- The response-versus-reaction model provides a clear message: response, which is a considered approach applying assertive behavior, is the most effective approach to find solutions, whereas reaction, which is instant and uses emotional fight-or-flight behavior, is unlikely to work.
- Within the response approach, there are a range of tactics, all based on applying a balance of driving and engagement behaviors.
- Resolving a conflict will invariably involve a negotiated agreement.

*(Reference Chapter 14)*


### Keeping the Supplier Engaged

- At the start of a contract, the supplier will be keen and enthusiastic.
- The challenge for the supplier manager is how to maintain that level of supplier enthusiasm for the duration of the engagement, which could be a 3-year contract.
- The supplier state model, based on energy level and attitude, provides a guide and checklist for assessing where a supplier currently sits.
- There is no magic solution to keeping the supplier engaged. Applying best practice and investing in the relationship will produce results; it must be worked at.
- The extensive checklist in Chapter 15 provides a range of ideas and actions to select from.

*(Reference Chapter 15)*


### Managing Exit

- Exit is part of the delivery phase of the lifecycle because service delivery must be maintained during the exit period.
- A parallel activity to the exit period could be a contract renewal based on an updated set of requirements; potentially, the process

goes back to step one of the lifecycle—identify requirements. It is good practice to formally go back to the lifecycle rather than just simply renewing on the basis of what was agreed 3 years ago.

- There are several possible situations and context to an exit, representing varying levels of risk to ongoing service delivery. Any exit represents a degree of risk and must be managed.
- The nine-point exit planner provides a map for managing the exit and the transition to the new arrangement, be it another supplier or a different delivery method—for example, in house.

*(Reference Chapter 16)*

## Summary of Reading List and Other References

References were cited within the text of each chapter; below is a summary of all references:

Fisher, R., and W. Ury. *Getting to Yes*. London, UK: Penguin. ISBN 9780140157352

Gupta, S. 2008. *Understanding Indian Culture and Bridging the Communication Gap*. London, UK: Subodh Gupta. ISBN 978-09556882-5-6

Hofstede, G, G. J. Hofstede, and M. Minkov. 2010. *Cultures and Organisations—Software of the Mind*. New York City, NY: McGraw-Hill Education. ISBN 978-0-07166418-9

Hofstede, G., G. J. Hofstede, M. Minkov. 2010. *Cultures and Organisations, Software of the Mind*, Third revised edition. New York City, NY: McGraw-Hill. ISBN 0-07-166418-1.

http://www.geerthofstede.eu

https://geerthofstede.com/research-and-vsm/dimension-data-matrix/

https://www.bernardmarr.com/default.asp (For KPQs)

Meyer, E. The Culture Map. New York City, NY: PublicAffairs. ISBN 978-1-61039 276-1

Mole, J. 2003. *Mind Your Manners*. Hachette, UK: Nicholas Brealey Publishing. ISBN 1-85788-314-4

Thomas, K. *Conflict Mode Instrument*. CPP. ISBN -13 978B0006SA349

# About the Author

*Richard Moxham* is a training consultant who has worked with clients in both corporate and public sectors in the United Kingdom and mainland Europe. Corporate clients represent a diverse range of commerce and industry, including banking, professional services, information technology, automotive, energy, aerospace, and transport. He works with clients in developing and delivering management and leadership development programs with strong contextual links to the client's business area, strategy, and culture. Over the last 12 years his work has increasingly been in the niche area of supplier management skills development. With the growth of outsourcing and offshoring in recent years, the need for organizations to have managers who are skilled and confident in managing strategic suppliers who are delivering mission-critical products and services to the business has become vitally important. For many managers, the move from leading in-house teams to managing external suppliers is a challenge; hence Richard's work in developing and facilitating learning workshops in this specialist area.

Prior to moving into consultancy and training, he had a progressive business career in sales and marketing, followed by time operations management, where he gained experience managing technology suppliers. His employment was mainly with U.S.-owned multinationals, including Nielsen, Proctor and Gamble, Xerox, Commerce Clearing House, and Lex Electronics.

# Index

# OTHER TITLES IN OUR SUPPLY AND OPERATIONS MANAGEMENT COLLECTION

Joy M. Field, Boston College, *Editor*

- *Moving the Chains: An Operational Solution for Embracing Complexity in the Digital Age* by Domenico LePore
- *The New Age Urban Transportation Systems, Volume I: Cases from Asian Economies* by Sundaravalli Narayanaswami
- *The New Age Urban Transportation Systems, Volume II: Cases from Asian Economies* by Sundaravalli Narayanaswami
- *Optimizing the Supply Chain* by Jay E. Fortenberry
- *Sustain: Extending Improvement in the Modern Enterprise* by W. Scott Culberson
- *Managing Using the Diamond Principle: Innovating to Effect Organizational Process Improvement* by Mark W. Johnson
- *Insightful Quality, Second Edition: Beyond Continuous Improvement* by Victor E. Sower and Frank K. Fair
- *The Global Supply Chain and Risk Management* by Stuart Rosenberg
- *Moving into the Express Lane: How to Rapidly Increase the Value of Your Business* by Rick Pay
- *The Effect of Supply Chain Management on Business Performance* by Milan Frankl
- *The High Cost of Low Prices: A Roadmap to Sustainable Prosperity* by David S. Jacoby
- *Sustainable Operations and Closed Loop Supply Chains, Second Edition* by Gilvan Souza
- *Statistical Process Control for Managers, Second Edition* by Victor Sower
- *Mastering Leadership Alignment: Linking Value Creation to Cash Flow* by Jahn Ballard and Andrew Bargerstock
- *Understanding the Complexity of Emergency Supply Chains* by Matt Shatzkin

## Announcing the Business Expert Press Digital Library

*Concise e-books business students need for classroom and research*

This book can also be purchased in an e-book collection by your library as

- *a one-time purchase,*
- *that is owned forever,*
- *allows for simultaneous readers,*
- *has no restrictions on printing, and*
- *can be downloaded as PDFs from within the library community.*

Our digital library collections are a great solution to beat the rising cost of textbooks. E-books can be loaded into their course management systems or onto students' e-book readers. The **Business Expert Press** digital libraries are very affordable, with no obligation to buy in future years. For more information, please visit **www.businessexpertpress.com/librarians**. To set up a trial in the United States, please email **sales@businessexpertpress.com**.

www.ingramcontent.com/pod-product-compliance
Lightning Source LLC
Chambersburg PA
CBHW061201220326
41599CB00025B/4568